杉森此馬英国留学日記

明治37年1月1日 - 12月31日

A Japanese Scholar's 1904 Diary in the UK.

安部規子編

海鳥社

カバー・表、本扉写真・杉森此馬（左）と右は平田喜一（禿木）と思われ、英国での撮影と思われる（柳川古文書館蔵「杉森此馬のアルバム」より）

杉森此馬のアルバム

　柳川古文書館に寄贈された「杉森此馬関連資料」には留学時の写真が含まれている。日記中には数回留学生仲間で写真撮影をしたとの記述がある。

　2月22日、鈴木禎次らとオックスフォードを訪問した際、案内してくれた平田喜一（禿木）と共にグループ写真を撮り、4月4日に平田からの写真を鈴木禎次を介して受け取っている。また、8月にニューカッスルオンタインを訪問中には8月27日と28日に同行者から写真を撮ってもらっている。11月12日には講義の後でグループ写真を撮ったとしており、受講者とともに写真館で記念撮影をしたかも知れない。

　上・左、右が杉森此馬。
　上・右、後列は左から杉森此馬、鈴木禎次、平田喜一（禿木）か。前列の2名は不明。
　下、後列左が杉森此馬
（グラビアの写真は全て，柳川古文書館蔵）

上の写真は、日記にロンドンの下宿先は「家族は夫婦に女子5人あり」と記述されていることから、ロンドンでの下宿先でのものかもしれない。杉森は後ろから2列目の左。右は杉森が親しくなった同宿のオーストリア人ドクトル・リットルである可能性も考えられる。下、次頁、杉森はロンドンでもオックスフォードでも親交のあった人々からよくお茶やピクニックに招かれており、これらの写真はそのような折に撮影されたものであろう。杉森の現地の人々との円満な人間関係が感じられる。

ロンドン大学で行われた外国人のための研修での記念写真。写真の裏には、「Holiday Course, London (For Foreigners) London University (Aug. 1905)」(1905は誤記か)と記されている。背景は Imperial Institute のエントランスと思われる。当該建物は現存していない。
杉森此馬は，前から2列目，左から6人目と思われる。

はじめに

安部規子

　この日記は，今から100年以上前の明治37（1904）年に杉森此馬によって書かれたものである。この年，杉森は文部省から英国に留学生として派遣されており，英国までの航海の様子とロンドン及びオックスフォードにおける留学生活が記録されている。

　日記帳は「明治三十七年当用日記」で，日付と曜日が予め印刷されており，自由に感想を書く10行の空欄の他に，天気と寒暖，発信，受信欄が設けられている。欄外にはその日あった歴史的な出来事などが印刷されている。例えば1月1日には「聖徳太子御生誕あり（敏達帝三年）」と記かれている。

　この日記帳は平成27（2015）年3月，杉森此馬の孫である髙月三世子氏により，杉森の出身地である福岡県柳川市にある柳川古文書館に寄贈された「杉森此馬関連資料」の一部である。

　目録によると，「杉森此馬関連資料」は，日記（A），履歴書類（B1～B9），辞令類（C1～C142），写真（D1～D208），妻である杉森ウメ関係文書（E1～E8）の5つに分類されている。

　髙月氏はこれらの資料を，アルバムの写真以外の文書のデジタル画像と共に寄贈された。日記についても全ページがデジタル化されており，もともとは小さな日記の手書きの記述を拡大して閲覧することができるようになった。

　この日記の大きな特徴として，1月1日から2月3日までの航海中の部分は日本語で，2月4日以降のロンドンでの留学生活は英語で書かれている点がある。

　英語で書いた理由としては，英語の修練という意味が大きかったと推察されるが，また同時に日本語と英語が混ざり合った文の不自然さを嫌う几

帳面さのためかもしれない。

　同時期の文部省留学生であった第五高等学校教授夏目金之助（漱石）が日記において，「四月三日（水）Glasgow University より examiner に appoint する由，公然通知あり。」といった日本語英語が混在した記述をしているのに対して，杉森は日記の日本語部分では英語の人名や地名にもカタカナを用い，「ブロードストリートステーション Broad Street Station よりハムステッドステーション Hampstead Heath Station 迄汽車に乗り6時頃スタンレーガーヅン44番 Stanley Gardens 44 ウォーコル氏 Mr. Walker 宅へ投宿す」と英語を添え書きしている。英語で表記する内容が圧倒的に多くなるロンドンでの生活が本格的に始まった時点で，全てを英語に変えたのかも知れない。

　本書では，言語に関わらず原文を左ページに，翻訳を右ページに配置している。

　巻末には「明治三十七年当用日記補遺」と「住所人名録」がついている。「補遺」にはその日のスペースでは書ききれなかった部分が記入されている。スエズ運河を通過する1月10日，マルセイユに上陸した1月18日，ハンプトンコートに出かけた5月15日，ストラットフォード・オン・エイボンを訪問した5月21日の4回である。

　日記の内容については日々の出来事だけが短く記されている日が多く，心中を吐露しているような記述は少ない。特に英語の部分では簡単な記述にとどまって日が多い。

　当時の日本と比較すれば，圧倒的に進んでいる英国に身を置き，驚きや感動と共に，当然劣等感，孤独感，葛藤といったものがあったはずであるが，日記からは，周囲と円満な人間関係を築き，愉快に毎日を過ごしている様子が感じられるばかりである。ここが夏目漱石の「ロンドン日記」とは大きく異なっている部分ではないだろうか。

　本書では，杉森此馬を当時の日本人留学生の1人の例として，明治時代後期の英国留学はどのようなものであったのかを知ることができる。またその中で杉森と交流があった人々の消息を示すこともできるであろう。

日記と共に「杉森此馬関連資料」に含まれる辞令とアルバムの写真の中から英国留学に関わるものを何点か示すこととする。

 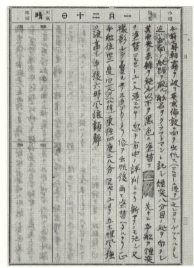

杉森此馬の日記、左・本扉、右・1月20日、煙突の図がある（柳川古文書館蔵）

杉森此馬英国留学日記●目次

はじめに　7

船上日記　明治37年1月1日-2月3日……………………………… 13

ロンドン滞在日記　2月4日-9月21日……………………………… 49

オックスフォード滞在日記　9月22日-12月31日……………………… 193

　住所人名録　261

　解説　267

　参考文献　280

　あとがき　283

凡例

1、原文の日本語部分はカタカナと漢字の縦書きで書かれているが、本書ではカタカナをひらがなにし、漢数字は算用数字に直し、難解な用語はルビをつけ、横書きとした。
2、原文には句読点がないが、読みやすいように句読点を入れ、適宜改行をほどこした。
3、読み取れない部分は□□□で示した。
4、英語部分で、明らかに間違っている綴り等は訂正した。
　オックスフォード大学の教員名の「セリンコート」は、諸資料を確認し、Selincourt とした。
5、英語表記で示された日本人名は、特定できた人物を除いてカタカナで表記した。
6、英語表現に誤りがあっても意味が読み取れる限りは原文通りとした。
7、同じものを対して異なる文字や表現が使われている場合は、ひとつの表現に統一した。
　「アフリカ」は「亜非利加」に統一した。
　シェイクスピアが生まれた町の名前は Stratford-on-Avon に統一した。
　「シェイクスピアの生家」は Shakespeare's Birthplace に統一した。
　『スケッチブック』は *The Sketch Book* に統一した。
　仕立て屋名である「チャペル」は Chappell に統一した。
8、天気、寒暖、発信、受信の欄は、記入内容がない日は欄の名前を削除した。なお、気温の表記は華氏である。
9、杉森自身が、英語部分で名前が思い出せない人物名を Mr. [　　] と空欄で示している場合がある。その場合の日本語訳は［氏名不明］と示した。
10、日露戦争関連で、英文の地名を特定できない場合は、和訳でも原文を使用した。
11、& c. / & C. は etcetera, and so on と同様に「など」という意味である。
12、金額の表記方法はいくつかある。例えば、4ポンド5シリング6ペンスの表記は「£4. 5s. 6d.」「£4-5-6」「£4/5/6」がある。1ポンドは20シリング、1シリングは12ペンスである。
13、和歌、漢詩は英訳していない分があり、詩の概要を英文でゴシックで示した。
14、当日の日記のスペースに書ききれず、巻末の補遺欄に追加して記述している日がある。補遺は4頁分あり、［補遺1頁に続く］のように示した。
15、文中の［注：　　］は編者による注である。
16、現在のイギリスの写真はすべて編者の撮影である。

船上日記

明治37年１月１日－２月３日

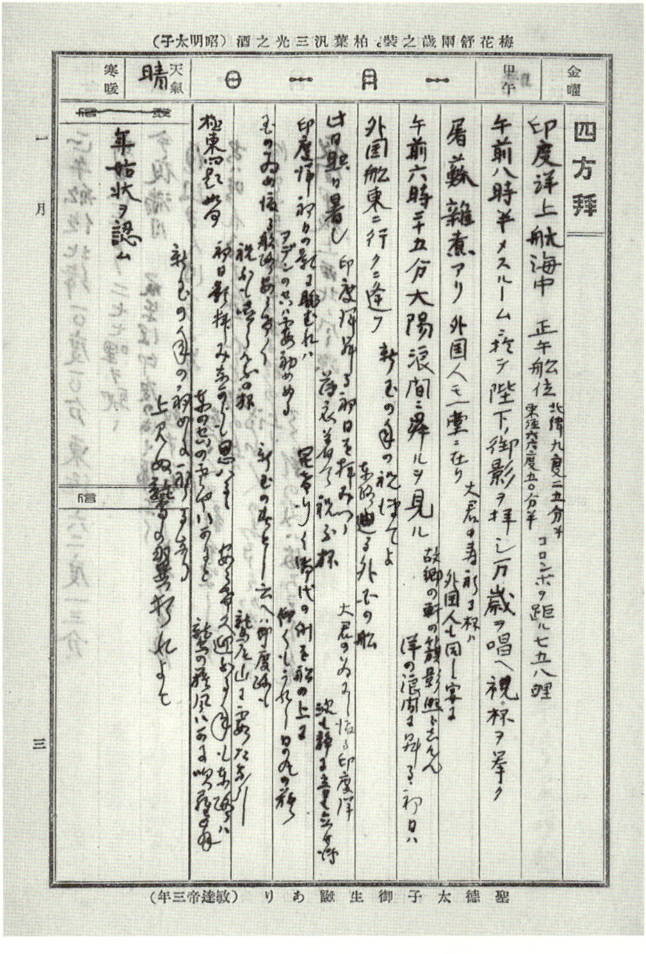

1月

　1月1日金曜　天気　晴
印度洋上航海中。正午船位、北緯9度25分半東経66度50分半。コロンボを距る758哩(マイル)。
午前8時半メスルームに於て陛下の御影(ぎょえい)を拝し万歳を唱え祝杯を挙ぐ。
屠蘇雑煮あり。外国人も一堂に在り。

　　大君の寿祀る杯は外国人も同じ宴に

午前6時25分太陽浪間に昇るを見る。

　　故郷の軒の旗影照ら志けん洋の浪間に昇る初日は

外国船東に行くに逢う。

　　新玉の年の祝伝えてよ東路廻る外国の船

此日照日暑し。

　　印度洋昇る初日を拝みつつ薄衣着て祝ふ杯
　　大君のためにし渡る印度洋浪も静に音も立せ傳(で)
　　印度洋初日の影に眺むればアデンの空は霞始める
　　開希ゆく御代の例を船の上に仰ぐもうれし日の丸の旗
　　国のため渡る航路安ら希く祝うも嬉しけふの杯
　　新玉の春とし言えば印度路も鷲尾山に霞たな引

極東問題如何。[注：朝鮮半島と満州の権益を巡って、日本とロシアが対立し、戦争直前の状況であった]

　　初日影拝みながらも思わるる東の空の雲やいかにと
　　安らけく迎ふる年も東路は鷲の旗風如何に吹羅舞(ふくらむ)

1月

1月1日金曜　天気　Fair

On the Indian Sea. The position of the ship at noon was lat. 9°25' N and long. 66°50' E.

The distance from Colombo was 758 miles.

At 8:30 a.m. respectfully looking at Emperor's portrait, we shouted "Banzai" and made a toast in the mess hall.

We had Japanese New Year's special drinks and food. Foreign passengers also celebrated in the same room.

A poem to describe the scene in which both Japanese and foreign passengers made a toast together to pray for Emperor's longevity.

At 6:25 a.m. saw the sun rise from among the waves.

> "This first sun will also shine on the national flag raised at the gate of my home on New Year's Day."

Met with a foreign ship sailing east.

> "Please, a foreign ship going east, bid a Happy New Year to my people."

It was hot today.

> "On the Indian Sea wearing summer clothes I look at the first sun of the year and make a toast."

新玉の年の初めに祀るなり上見ぬ鷲の翼折れよと

年始状を認む。

　　1月2日土曜　天気　晴
正午船位、北緯10度10分東経62度13分
前日正午より277哩を馳す。
今夜満月。

　　筑紫潟印度の海も隔なく照らすは於奈じけふの望月
　　酒酌まん波間に昇る望月に故郷人の影を写して
　　空は晴れ月は満つれど船の上は訪ふ人のなきぞ悲しき
　　何事も足らぬがちなる船の上も月影のみは満ちわたりけり

夜間甲板上西北の風涼し。

　　1月3日日曜　天気　晴
　正午船位、北緯10度55分東経57度19分。前日正午より292哩を馳す。西北の風涼し。

　　1月4日月曜　天気　晴
　午前6時右舷遥かにソコトラ島を認む。又近くブロゾルアイランヅを見る。共にテーブルランドの好標本とす。船員はブロゾルアイランヅを軍艦島と云うものあり。形二艘の軍艦に酷似す。前月31日ミニコイ島の灯台を

Five poems are added to express his determination and celebration of the New Year's Day.

What is happening regarding Far East issues?

Three poems are written to imply political issues with Russia.

Wrote New Year's cards.

1月2日土曜　天気　Fair
The position of the ship at noon: lat. 10°10'N and long. 62°13' E.
The distance sailed since yesterday noon: 277 miles.
Tonight a full moon.

Four poems are written expressing his admiration for the beautiful full moon amidst his loneliness of having no friends to enjoy the views.

At night on the deck the northwest wind was cool.

1月3日日曜　天気　Fair
The position of the ship at noon: lat. 10°55'N and long. 57°19' E. The distance sailed since yesterday noon: 292 miles. The wind from the northwest was cool.

1月4日月曜　天気　Fair
At 6 a.m. far to starboard saw Socotra Island, and also closer Two Brothers Islands. Both are good examples of tableland. Some sailors call the latter "Warship Islands." Their shape looked like two warships. It

見てより初めて陸地を見る。

正午船位、北緯10度48分東経52度27分。前日正午より293哩を馳す。

午後5時亜非利加(アフリカ)洲の東北端グヮーダフィー岬の前を過ぐ。山形悉く大テーブルランドとす。蓋(けだ)し亜非利加沼岸(ママ)の特性なり。初めて亜細亜以外の大陸を見し。

夜間西北の風涼し。

1月5日火曜　天気　晴

日出午前6時30分。東北追風にて暑し。

正午船位、北緯12度26分東経47度26分、前日正午よ297哩を馳す。

1月6日水曜　天気　晴

午前7時半バベルマンデブ海峡に入る。ペリム島を近く左舷に見て過ぐ。左に遠く亜非利加大陸を望み、右に近く亜剌比亜(アラビア)西南端を見る。ペリム島と亜非利加の間を大狭と云い亜剌比亜との間を小狭と云う。昼間は小狭を過ぎ夜間は大狭を過ぐ。此島は英国の石炭貯蔵地にして又要塞地とす。灯台あり又砲台あり此島も赤たテーブルランド的にして他にも幾個の大長屋の屋根の如き島あり。

本船より信号旗を挙げて日露関係の事を聞きたるに、"No war is declared." の返信号を見る。

此海峡は則ち亜剌比亜海より紅海に入るの関門とす。船は殆ど北の方向を取る。南風強く波甚だ高し。

　　あさぼらけ青海原を眺むれば白波高き紅の海

午前10時、亜剌比亜海岸にモッカ港を遠見す。所謂モッカ珈琲の産地とす。

正午船位、北緯13度38分東経42度56分。前日正午より307哩を馳す。気

was the first land we had seen since the end of last month when we saw the lighthouse on Minicoy Island.

The position of the ship at noon: lat. 10°48' N and long. 52°27'E. The distance sailed since yesterday noon: 293 miles.

At 5 p.m. passed Cape Guardafui northeast end of Africa. The mountains are all huge tableland in shape. It is certainly a trait of African coast. Saw a continent other than Asia for the first time.

During the evening the wind from the northwest was cool.

1月5日火曜　天気　Fair

Sunrise at 6:30 a.m. Had a tail wind from the northeast and was hot.

The position of the ship at noon: lat. 12°26' N and long. 47°26' E. The distance sailed since yesterday noon: 297 miles.

1月6日水曜　天気　Fair

At 7:30 a.m. entered Bab el Mandeb. The ship passed near Perim Island to port. On the far left side was the African Continent, and a little closer on the right was the southwest end of Arabia. The gorge between Perim Island and Africa is called Big Gorge and the one between the island and Arabia, Small Gorge. During the daytime passed the small one and at night passed the big one. This island functions as a coal storage and also as a fort for Britain. With a lighthouse and firebase, this island is also a kind of tableland, and there are several other islands which look like the long roofs of big terrace houses.

Raising a signal flag, the ship asked about the Japan-Russia situation and got a reply "No war has been declared." This strait is the gateway to the Red Sea from the Arabian Sea. The ship now sailed almost north. Had strong south wind and rather high waves.

"In the morning looking at the blue sea with white high waves, we

温80度海水略同じ。
　午後2時アブ島を近く右舷に見て過ぐ。此島はトルコ（？）領の小なる岩島にして灯台あれども政府財政困難のためか当時点火せずと云う。今夜室内暑し。

　　1月7日木曜　天気　晴
　風静に波極て穏なり。紅海は印度洋よりも暑しと聞き居りたれども左程暑からず。甲板上朝風心地よく海上霞亙りて春の如し。
　正午船位、北緯17度49分東経40度4分。前日正午より302哩を馳す。午後、風全く去りて海面油を注げるか如く苦熱甚し。今夜日本料理あり。飯汁、刺身、輝焼、甘煮、香物美味云うべからず。

　　1月8日金曜　天気　晴
　北風にて甲板上北風涼に過ぐれども室内は暑し。正午船位、北緯22度2分東経37度40分。前日正午より287哩を馳す。地図上にては紅海と云うは狭き海の様なれども前日も今日も陸地は勿論小島だに見えず。

sail into the Red Sea."

At 10 a.m. in the distance saw Mocha Port on Arabian coast. This is the place where mocha coffee is produced. The position of the ship at noon: lat. 13°38' N and long. 42°56' E. The distance sailed since yesterday noon: 307 miles. The temperature was 80° and that of the sea water was almost the same.

At 2 p.m. the ship passed Abu Island close to starboard. This island is a small rock on Turkish(?) territory, and had a lighthouse but because of the financial problems of the government, it cannot afford to light the beacon lamp, I heard. It is hot in the room tonight.

1月7日木曜　天気　Fair

The wind is quiet and the waves quite calm. I heard that it is hotter on the Red Sea than on the Indian Sea, but it isn't that hot. The morning wind on the deck was refreshing and a mist hung over the sea as if in spring.

The position of the ship at noon: lat. 17°49' N and long. 40°04' E. The distance sailed since yesterday noon: 302 miles. In the afternoon had no wind and the surface of the sea looked shiny as if oil were poured, it being intensely hot. For dinner Japanese food was served. Rice, soup, sashimi, broiled or sweetly cooked dishes, and pickles, were all very delicious.

1月8日金曜　天気　Fair

Had north wind and on the deck it was too cool but it was hot in the room. The positon of the ship at noon: lat. 22°02' N and long. 37°40' E. The distance sailed since yesterday noon: 287 miles. Although on the map the Red Sea looks narrow, no land or even an island was seen yesterday and

1月9日土曜　天気　晴

　日出6時50分、北風涼し。船は既に温帯に入る。12月9日より熱帯中に在る事30日。今再び温帯に入る。左舷遠く亜非利加沿岸を見る。

　正午船位、北緯26度23分東経34度54分。前日正午より302哩。

1月10日日曜

　日出7時4分。俄かに寒冷となり人皆更衣に忙はし。午前9時スエズ着。検疫官来りて検疫す。カナル［注：運河］通過の準備をなす。（楫に鉄板を附し楫面を広大にす）。

　土人（土耳古人）来りて煙草、干無花果、エルサレムカンラ樹細工物等を売る。船子には亜非利加土人もあり。印度人より一層黒く、真の黒坊なり。土耳古人は所謂土耳古帽を戴き筒袖に女学生袴の如きものを着く。午後12時30分水先案内乗船。ポルトサイドに向ふ。全45分カナルに入る。

　カナルは幅30間許。ポルトサイド迄88哩とす。1859年エヂプト王サイドの時工を起し1869年工を終る。実に世界の大工事とす。技士レセップの名カナルと共に永久没すべからず。可惜、パナマ工事に失敗し、不名誉に世を終る。銅像は空しくポルトサイドの埠頭に立つのみ。［補遺1頁に続く］カナルを通過するには船の大小により異なれども河内丸の如きは片道凡そ1万8千円を払ふものとす。カナルは株式会社スエズカナル会社の有にして利益極て多し。従って通過料も前年よりも減せりと云ふ。

　船は平均5哩（平常12哩）の速力にて進行すれども処により極て緩行する処あり。之を通過するに17時間を要す。左方1哩許に旧スエズあり。一小市とす。此処より汽車ありて「ポルトサイド」「カイロ」等に到るを得。「カイロ」には「イスメイリヤ」より分岐す。「カナル」の左右は砂漠にて右は所謂亜刺比亜の大砂漠に続くものにして左は「ナイル」河を距てて亜

today.

1月9日土曜　天気　Fair

　Sunrise at 6:50. Cool north wind. The ship was already in the temperate zone. After 30 days in the tropical zone since Dec. 9th, we are now in the temperate zone again. Saw the coast of Africa in the distance to port.

　The position of the ship at noon: lat. 26°23' N and long. 34°54' E. The distance sailed since yesterday noon: 302 miles.

1月10日日曜

　Sunrise at 7:04. It got chilly suddenly and people were busy changing clothes. At 9 a.m. arrived in Suez. Quarantine staff came to inspect. Got ready to pass the Canal. (An iron plate was attached to the rudder to make the surface bigger.) The local people (Turkish) came to sell cigarettes, dried figs, Jerusalem plant handicrafts, and so on. Some seamen were African. They looked darker than Indians and truly black. Turkish people wore what we call Turkish caps, straight-sleeved jackets and something like hakama, or long pleated skirts, for Japanese girl students. At 12:30 p.m. a pilot got onboard. Set sail for Portsaid. At 12:45 entered the Canal.

　The Canal is about 54 meters wide. It was 88 ms to Portsaid. The construction started in 1859 under the reign of Egyptian King Said and ended in 1869. It was truly great construction work in the world. The name of the engineer Lesseps, together with the Canal, should not be lost forever. What a shame. He failed in constructing the Panama Canal and died in dishonor. The statue stands on the pier in Portsaid in vain. [Continue to Appendix p. 1] In order to pass the canal, a ship like this the Kawachi Maru is to pay about 18,000 yen for one way, but it depends on the ship size. The Canal is owned by Suez Canal Company Ltd. who

非利加の大砂漠に通す。左右渺茫(びょうぼう)たる砂原一木一石を見ず。僅かに一種の雑草の処々にあるを見るのみ。土人居宅のある処に駱駝数頭あるを見たり。

　3時15分ビットル湖に入る。5時25分再びカナルに入る。日暮れソルチライトにて前路を輝す。6時船底浅所に触れ船体大に左舷に傾き人皆愕きたれども直に離礁事なきを得たり。停船数分時にして忽ち進航す。7時15分チムサ湖に入る。湖辺にイスメイリアと云う小市あり。エジプトのパシャ此処に住す。水先案内小蒸気にて来り先きに本船に乗り居りたるものと交代す。此湖は小なるものなるを以て忽ち復カナルに入る。

　　鑿山穿豁水路通
　　東西船泊由此路
　　丈夫所貴独心事
　　埠頭空聳偉人像

　　火輪蹴波幾鵬程
　　春去夏過秋将暮
　　東西両洋従是分
　　天邊遥見西乃山

　　1月11日月曜　天気　晴
　午前5時ポルトサイド着（日出6時50分）此処にては夜昼の区別なく着船するや否や石炭船来りて石炭を積込むものなるに石炭船来らず。浮説(ふせつ)紛々日露開戦の説盛なり。10時出帆の予定なりしも12時になりても出帆は勿論石炭船も来らず。愈(いよいよ)日露開戦［注：実際の開戦は、1904年（明治37年）2月8日］したるにより石炭積込みを拒絶したるものならんとの想像説

makes a huge profit. Therefore the toll became lower than last year, I heard.

The ship sailed at an average speed of five miles per hour (usually 12 miles) but in some spots it sailed extremely slowly. It took 17 hours to pass the Canal. About one mile away on the left side was the former Suez, which is now a small city. From here trains are available and people can get to Portsaid, Cairo and so on. The way to Cairo diverges at Ismailia. On both sides of the Canal are the deserts: the right side leads to the great desert of Arabia and the left, across the Nile, a great desert of Africa. On both sides are endless sandy plains with no trees or no rocks. Only a certain kind of weed could be seen here and there. Saw some camels at the local people's homes.

At 3:15 entered Bitter Lake. At 5:25 went back to the Canal. The sun set and the way in front was illuminated by a search light. At 6 the ship bottom touched the shallows and the ship sharply tilted to port, which surprised the passengers, but refloated again immediately safely. After stopping for some minutes, the ship began to sail again. At 7:15 the ship entered Lake Timsah. On the lake shore is a small city called Ismailia. The Egyptian pasha lives here. A pilot came on a small steam boat and replaced the predecessor. This lake is a small one and the ship soon entered the Canal again.

A Chinese style poem to express the admiration of the Canal.

1月11日月曜　天気　Fair

At 5 a.m. arrived in Portsaid (sunrise at 6:50). Here night and day as soon as a ship arrives a coal carrier comes to fill it with coal, but this time a carrier never came. Various rumors were afloat and among them was the outbreak of war between Japan and Russia. The ship was scheduled to set sail at 10, but even at 12 a coal carrier didn't come, not

起る。午後石炭船来り石炭は積込たれども出帆の模様なし。

　船長上陸、本社に向け船の進退を問う。是れ愈開戦旦夕（たんせき）に迫り居るとすれば地中海にて露艦に捕拿さるる恐れあるが為なり。夜に入るも返電来らず。浮説は浮説を生じ船中何となく穏ならず。限りある船中にて浮説の起るは解し難き事の様なれども既に10日を以て開戦せりとか旅順附近にて衝突せりとか、アルヂェンチン共和国より買入れたる２艘の軍艦は現時ヂェノアに在りて本船の水火夫は夫れに乗遷り本船は外国水火夫を雇入れロンドンに行くとか想像停止する処を知らざるものの如し。

　深更（しんこう）に到るも返電来らず。船は勿論出帆せず。種々なる想像談をなしながら寝に就く。此日終に上陸せず。

　ポルトサイドはカナルの尽る処にして西洋と東洋を混和したる処なり。人気極て悪しく市街清潔なれども小なり。人の手にて植られたものの外樹木なし。屋根の上に木を植たる家あるを見たり。レセップの銅像は埠頭に立らる。杖、煙草、エヂプト製ダンツー、エルサレムカンラン細工物等を売来る。

　元日認めたる年始状を此処にて発郵す。

１月12日火曜日　天気　晴

　午前１時30分解纜（かいらん）（マルセーユ迄行けの返信ありたり）。人皆安堵の思をなす。然れども浮説は尚止まず。露国戦闘艦２艘巡洋艦水雷艇数艘を率い東洋に向かうもの今地中海に在り。途中にて逢うならんと云う説あり。

to mention even setting sail. Some imagined that because of the war outbreak, the loading of coal must have been rejected. In the afternoon a coal carrier came and coal was loaded but there was no sign of setting sail.

The captain landed to ask the head office whether to leave or not. It was because the ship could be captured by a Russian warship in the Mediterranean if the war was really about to break out. Even when night came, there was no reply. There were groundless rumors one after another and the atomosphere in the ship wasn't calm. I didn't know why these rumors were afloat in the isolated space in the ship but somehow people couldn't stop making up stories: the war already broke out on the 10th, or there was a military conflict near Port Arthur, or the two warships bought from the Argentine Republic being at present in Genoa, our seamen and firemen would board them and this ship would hire foreign seamen and firemen to leave for London. Their imagination seemed to be endless. As the night advanced, no reply came. The ship, needless to say, never set sail. People went to bed, talking about various stories they invented. This day eventually we didn't land.

Portsaid is where the Canal ends and the West and the East meet. The city didn't look nice at all, and the streets were clean but small. There were no trees except for those planted by people. Saw houses with trees planted on the roofs. The statue of Lesseps stands on the pier. Local people came to sell sticks, cigarettes, Egyptian carpets, Jerusalem olivine handicrafts and so on.

Posted here the cards I had written on New Year's Day.

1月12日火曜日　天気　Fair

At 1:30 a.m. weighed anchor (had a reply that the ship should go to Marseille). All the people felt relieved. However groundless rumors didn't stop: two Russian warships with several cruisers and torpedo boats

ポルトサイド出帆後開戦したらんには本船は必ず捕拿されん等の想像説復起る。愈捕虜となりてオデッサに行ならん程と雑談せり。
　7時雨降り波高く船動揺す。少時にして雨止む。9時半左舷前方遥に黒煙盛に起る。双眼鏡を以て見れば4本マスト煙突4個慥に軍艦なり。本船は遽に煙突8分目以下を薄色（元黒）に塗替え、舳の船名を塗抹す。先に対馬丸が地中海にて露国水雷艇に追尾され煙突を塗替え逃れたりなどと聞き居たるも今は我身の上となるも可笑。前方の船は次第に近く愈接近するに及び英国軍艦なるを認めたり。斯かる時節には随分滑稽の事もあるものなり。正午船位、北緯32度9分東経30度47分ポルトサイドより103哩。此日夜に到るも波高船動揺止まず。

　1月13日水曜日　天気　晴
　日出7時12分波平なり。正午船位、北緯33度50分東経22度五5分。前日正午より266哩。右舷遠くクリート島を見る。山上雪白し。午後八時右舷にクリート西南端の灯台を見る。

　1月14日木曜日　天気　晴れ　寒暖　55°
　The position of the ship 35°－55'N, 20°－29'E.
　Distance run 296ms. Therm. 55°

heading for the East were in the Mediterranean at the moment and they would find this ship on the way. The supposition rose again that once the war began after it had left Portsaid, this ship would surely be captured. People said they would be sent to Odessa as captives.

At 7 a.m. with rainfall and high waves, the ship rolled and pitched. The rain stopped soon. At 9:30 far to port saw a lot of black smoke rising. With a binocular, saw a ship with four masts and four chimneys, which was surely a warship. This ship immediately painted the lower part of the chimney in light color (originally black) and erased the ship name on the bow. Had once heard a Japanese ship Tsushima Maru was pursued by Russian torpedo boats in the Mediterranean and managed to escape by repainting the chimneys. It was funny that the same thing was happening to us. As the ship in front got nearer and nearer, we found that it was a British warship. In this political situation, such a ridiculous incident happened. The position of the ship at noon: lat. 32°09' N and long. 30°47' E. The distance from Portsaid: 103 miles. On this day even at night the waves were still high and the ship was shaky.

1月13日水曜日　天気　Fair

Sunrise at 7:12. The waves calm. The position of the ship at noon: lat. 33°50' N and long. 22°55' E. The distance sailed since yesterday noon: 266 miles. Far to the starboard saw Crete Island. The summit was white with snow. At 8 p.m. saw a lighthouse on the southwest end of Crete to starboard.

1月14日木曜日　天気　Fair　寒暖　55°

The position of the ship 35°55'N, 20°29'E.
Distance run 296 miles. Therm. 55°

1月15日金曜　天気　晴

　日出7時25分。日出つれば前方既に伊太利(イタリア)及シシリー島を見る。エトナ山峯積雪山腹に及ぶ。此山は昔時地中海の灯台と云われたる大火山なりしも今は噴火せず。

　11時船は北向メッシナ海峡に入る。右に伊太利レッグ市を見、左にシシリー島メッシナ市を見る。両陸相距る甚だ近く、美観云ふべからず。12時海峡の最狭所を過ぐ。馬関［注：下関］門司間過ぐるが如し。船は再び西北に向ひ外洋に出ず。正午船位、北緯36度18分東経15度39分。前日正午より287哩。

　午後3時スツロンボリー島を近く右舷に見る。富士山形の小島にして火山なり。頂上に雲あり。噴火の状を見ざるを遺憾とす。山麓に温泉ありと云ふ。30軒内外の人家を認む。（宇品湾似の島に似たり）

1月16日土曜　天気　晴後雨

　前夜来波高く船動揺す。午前11時半前方遥にサルヂニア島の山峯を見る。

　正午船位、北緯40度37分東経10度58分。前日正午より258哩。午後降雨。夜に入り益甚し。門司出帆以来雨らしき雨は之を始めとす。サルヂニア島とコルシカ島の間ボシファノ海峡を通ふるを順路とすれども波高く夜暗く危険なるが為めコルシカ島と大陸との間を通過せり為めにマルセーユ着港は12、3時間の遅着となる。終夜波高く甲板上を越すこと数回。

1月15日金曜　天気　Fair

　Sunrise at 7:25. Saw in front Sicily Island, Italy, at the sunrise. The snow covering Mt. Etna extended to its side. This mountain used to be a great volcano called the lighthouse of the Mediterranean but now it doesn't erupt.

　At 11 the ship directed north and entered the Strait of Messina. Saw Lecce City in Italy on the right side and Messina on Sicily on the left side. Both lands were so close and I couldn't find words to describe the beauty. At noon the ship passed the narrowest part of the strait. It was as if we were passing between Bakan and Moji in Japan. The ship again went northwest and went into the open sea. The position of the ship at noon: lat. 36°18' N and long. 15°39' E. The distance sailed since yesterday noon: 287 miles.

　At 3 p.m saw Stromboli Island close to starboard. It is a small island and volcano shaped like Mt. Fuji. Clouds were seen on the peak. It was a pity it was not erupting. Heard that there were hot springs on the foot of the mountain. Recognized some thirty houses. (Looked like an island in Ujina Bay in Hiroshima.)

1月16日土曜　天気　Fair then rainy

　Since last night the high waves have made the ship shaky. At 11:30 far in front saw the summits of Sardinia Island.

　The position of the ship at noon: lat. 40°37' N and long. 10°58' E. The distance sailed since yesterday noon: 258 miles. Had rain in the afternoon. At night had heavy rain. This is the first time that we have had real rainfall since we left Moji. Passing the Strait of Bosifano between Sardinia Island and Corsica Island was a usual route but at the moment it was dangerous this time with high waves and darkness, so the route between Corsica Island and the continent was chosen. Therefore the arrival at Marseille Port was expected to be 12 or 13 hours behind

１月17日日曜　天気　雨後晴

夜来風雨強く怒濤如山(どとうやまのごとし)。船体動揺甚し。後雨止みたれども風強く波高し。前方右舷に仏国の山峯雪を頂けるを見る。空気強からず。55度くらいとす。正午船位、北緯43度1分東経7度39分。前日正午より264哩。午後空全く晴れ波静なり。午後3時1帆船より進行力を失す助力を乞うの信号あり。本船は忽ち回航。ボートを卸し其の船に到り事情を問わしむ。帆船は伊太利国商船にて前夜マルセーユより引船にて来りたるものなれども風波のため引綱切け互に相失したるなりと云う（ママ）。マルセーユにて其の船の本社に事情を電報し呉れよとの依頼を受け、其の船を遣し本船は再びマルセーユに向う。頗(すこぶ)る不得要領の件なりし。

　日没4時45分。

１月18日月曜　天気　晴　寒暖　氷を見る

　午前2時マルセーユ港外に停船す。日出7時40分。気温32度。空気頗る強し。甲板上より港市を望めばノートルダム［注：大聖堂］は最高の丘上に聳え港内処々に砲台あり。大廈高楼(たいかこうろう)は朝霧の中に隠見(いんけん)し壮観云ふべからず。船長船医ボートにて検疫所に到る。検疫員来りて消毒す。終て進航ドックに入る。此処のドックは広大且つ完全なるものにて実に世界一二に位すと称せらる（ハムブルグを第一とす）橋梁数条あり。船到れば橋は回転して道を開き船の通行を自在にす。ドック中幾多の大船巨泊悉く岸に横着けにす。

　昼飲後上陸。始めて欧州の土を踏む。市街を散歩しノートルダム（Our

schedule. All night the waves were high and came over the deck several times.

1月17日日曜　天気　Rainy then fair

During the night had heavy rain and mountainous waves. The ship rolled and pitched heavily. The rain stopped later but the wind was strong and the waves were high. In front of us to starboard were mountains in France covered with snow. The atmosphere was quiet. It was around 55.° The position of the ship at noon: lat. 43°01' N and long. 07°39' E. The distance sailed since yesterday noon: 264 miles. In the afternoon the sky was clear and the waves were calm. At 3 p.m. received a signal from a sailing ship that they had lost power and needed help. This ship turned immediately. A boat was lowered to ask about their condition. The sailing ship was an Italian merchant ship and was tugged by a tugboat from Marseille last night but due to the storm the towrope was cut and both got lost. Asked to send a telegram at Marseille to their main office to inform them of its condition, this ship started for Marseille leaving the ship. This was really an unclear case.

Sunset at 4:45

1月18日月曜　天気　Fair　寒暖　Saw ice

At 2 a.m. the ship stopped outside Marseille Port. Sunrise at 7:40. Temperature 32°. The atmosphere was very strong. Looked at the port city from the deck, and found Notre Dame at the summit on the hill and also saw firebases in several places in the port. Big and high-rise buildings in the morning mist looked magnificent. The captain and the doctor went to Quarantine station by boat. Quarantine staff came to disinfect the ship. After that the ship went into dock. The dock here is so huge and perfect that it is regarded as the first or second best in the world (Hamburg is arguably number one). There were several bridges.

Lady　屋上高くマリアの像を安置する旧教会堂）に昇る。ノートルダムは市中最高の所に在り。見下せば市街港湾一目の内に集まり極て壮観なり。丘は一千尺もあらん。マリアの金像は堂の頂上に輝く堂内を見写真を買い、［補遺２頁につづく］昇降機にて市街に下る。雨も市中散歩。試に、バール（飲食店）にて葡萄酒を呑む。極て廉なり。始め葡萄酒と云う事解らず。葡萄を紙片に画き示したれば葡萄の砂糖漬を持来る。手を振て其否らざるを示し更に之を絞る様を示せばシャンパンを持来る。之れではならぬと思いBordeauxと書き示したれば始めて葡萄酒を持来たる。

　９時帰船す。市中バールの多き事驚くべき数にて夏時東京の氷店より多し。大なるは２、３００人を容るに足る。何れも殆ど満員の有様にて頗る遊惰の風あり。上海の公煙茶楼に類す仏国の前途も略兆すべし。

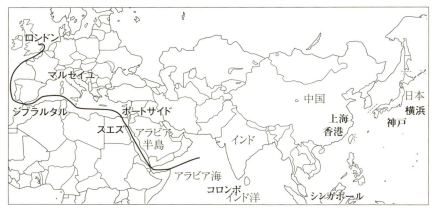

明治期の日本郵船の欧州航路（「門司を出帆以来」と１月16日に記したのみで、国内の寄港地、インド洋までは日記にはない。実線部分が日記に記されている航路）

１月19日火曜　天気　晴

　朝食後、市街散歩、美術館を見る。構造堅牢、前面噴水彫刻の意匠見事なり。室内絵画彫刻頗る巧妙なり。裸体画も此に至て神聖とも真美とも云うべし。

　12時帰船。午後再び上陸。カセドラル［注：ノートルダム大聖堂］を見る（外部）。旧ドックに到る途中 狭隘 きょうあい の巷を過ぐ。更に転じて稍広き処 やや に出つ。数多の婦人出来り、突然帽を奪いて去る。之を取返さんとて室内に

When ships approach, they turn to open the way for them to pass. In the dock were several huge ships and all of them were drawn to the coast.

After lunch landed. Set foot on European soil for the first time. Took a walk in the city and ascended to Notre Dame (Our Lady, an old cathedral where the statue of Maria is enshrined high on the roof). Notre Dame is located on the highest hill in the city. Looking down from there, you can see the whole city and the port, and it is truly spectacular. The hill probably was 300 meters high. Looked inside the cathedral, on the top of which the golden Maria statue stands, bought some pictures, [to be continued to Appendix p.2], and went down to the city by lift. Walked around the city in the rain. To give it a try, had wine at a bar. Very cheap. I ordered wine, but at first I couldn't make myself understood. When I drew grapes on a piece of paper, syrupped grapes were served. By waving a hand, showed it was not what I ordered. I did gestures of squeezing grapes and champaign was brought. Found this did not work, and only after I wrote "Bordeaux" and showed it, wine was served.

At 9 returned to the ship. Surprised at the number of bars in the city. More bars than shaved ice shops in Tokyo in summer. Big ones can accommodate two or three hundred people. All of them were almost full and people looked lazy and idle. It looked similar to public smoking and tea houses in Shanghai, China, and the future of France should be much the same.

1月19日火曜日　天気　Fair

After breakfast took a walk around the city and visited art galleries. Sturdy structures and the design of the fountains in front of the architecture were brilliant. The paintings and sculptures displayed inside were ingenious. Nude pictures could be said sacred and truly beautiful.

At noon returned to the ship. Landed again in the afternoon. Saw the cathedral (outside). On the way to the old dock, passed narrow streets,

はいれば忽ち内より鎖して復出べからず。同行3人のものも女軍に取囲まれ外より戸を開かんとすれども能はず。幸にして巡査来りたれば戸を開き出るを得たり。危険極まれりと云うべし。

　旧ドック通に出て同行、双眼鏡を買う。双眼鏡は此市の名産なりと云う。郵便を出し帰船す。此市の家の構造は立派なれども市街は一般に不潔なり。往来の男女亦衣服きたなし。

　　発信　自宅其他へ書状を出す（VIA アメリカにて）
　　　　倫敦茨木氏書状1
　　　　　ロンドン
　　　　伯林戸田氏へ書状1
　　　　　ベルリン

　　1月20日水曜　天気　晴
　午前7時朝霧を破り英京倫敦に向て出帆す（マルセーユ港を）。之れよりヂブラルタル迄は西南の航路を取る。船名をクラフトマンと記し煙突8分目の処を白くし其中央に赤条を施し以下を黒色に塗替う。

　先きに本船が煙突を塗替マルセーユに入港するや忽ち市中の評判となり新聞にも記しまた撮影して売るものすらありたり。依て出帆後再び塗替へたるなり。正午船位、42度41分（北緯）東経4度28分。マルセーユより57哩。風強く浪高し。午後6時風浪鎮静。

煙突塗替えの図

　　1月21日木曜　天気　晴
　日出7時20分。船西南に進むに従い気候稍温暖を加う。午前8時左舷に2個の鯨を見る。マチョルカ島及びイヴィザ島を遠く左舷に見る。正午船位、北緯38度49分東経0度32分。前日正午より296哩。右舷近く西班牙国
　　　　　　　　　　　　　　　　　　　　　　　　　　　　　スペイン
Nao岬及附近沿岸を見る。午後7時パロス港附近の灯台を見る。

and then came to an open place. Several women came out and they ran away taking my hat. The moment I went into the house in order to get it back, they locked me inside and I couldn't get out. Three people in the group were also surrounded by the women, and couldn't unlock the door. Fortunately, a policeman came along and he opened the door. I managed to get out. It was really a dangerous experience.

Coming out to the old dock street, one of us bought binoculars. I hear binoculars were noted products here. Posted letters letters and returned to the ship. The house structures were fine here but the city streets were generally unclean. Both men and women in the street wore dirty clothes.

1月20日水曜　天気　Fair

At 7 a.m. in the middle of morning mist the ship left (Port Marseille) for London, the capital of Britain. From here to Gibraltar the ship took a southwest route. Represented the ship name as Craftman, painted the lower part of the chimney white, with a red line in the center, the rest black.

Earlier as soon as it changed chimney color in entering the port, the ship became popular and was reported on the newspaper and some people took its pictures to sell. Therefore after the departure, it was repainted. The position of the ship at noon: lat. 42°41' N and long. 4°28' E. The distance sailed from Marseille: 57 miles. The wind was strong and the waves were high. At 6 p.m. the wind and waves became calm.

1月21日木曜　天気　Fair

Sunrise at 7:20. As the ship sailed in the southwest, it became warmer and warmer. At 8 a.m. to port saw two whales. Saw Mallorca Island and Ibiza Island far to the port. The position of the ship at noon was lat. 38°49' N and long. 0°32' E. The distance sailed since yesterday noon was

1月22日金曜　天気　晴

　気暖なり。西班牙の山峯（シェラ子バダ？）は雪を戴くを見る。正午船位、北緯36度16分西経４度44分。前日正午より318哩。午後２時30分左舷に亜非利加を見、右舷に近くヂブラルタルの要塞地を見る。山の高さ凡そ１千56百呎悉く岩石より成り実に天然の大砲台とす。東は紅海のペリム島西は此ヂブラルタルを守れば紅海、地中海の全権は全く英国の手中にありて１隻の敵艦を入るを得ず又出るを得ず。

　此日風強く波極て高し。然れども風順なるを以て船動揺せず。数多のイルカ船の周囲に跳躍。３時半ヂブラルタル海峡最狭（４哩許）の所を過ぐ。11日ポルトサイド着以来地中海にある事12日間。今即ち大西洋に入る之より船は西北の方向を取る。風波静なり。午後６時右舷にトラフォルガル岬の灯台を見る。ネルソン戦没の当時を思はざるものなし。

　1月23日土曜　天気　晴

　日出７時25分。午前６時右舷近くヴィンセント岬を見る。岬は幾里に亙る一字状の丘の尽る所にして此所に一の寺院ありモンク住す。此寺院はトラフォルガル戦役の時ネルソンの遺骸を持来りたる処なりと云ふ。

　船は之れより次第に北の方向を取る。正午船位、北緯38度６分西経９度26分。前日正午より294哩。午後２時半ポルチュガル国ロカ岬を近く右舷に見る。此岬の東南に狭き湾あり、湾の尽る処はタグス河口にして首府リ

296 miles. Near to starboard saw Cape Nao, Spain, and the coast. At 7 a.m. saw a lighthouse near Port Paros.

1月22日金曜　天気　Fair

The climate was warm. Saw the mountain peaks in Spain (Sierra Nevada?) covered with snow. The postion of the ship at noon: lat. 36°16' N and long. 4°44' W. The distance sailed since yesterday noon: 318 miles. At 2:30 p.m. saw Africa to starboard, and the fortress in Gibraltar to port. The mountains were approximately 1500 to 1600 feet high and all made up of rocks, which make natural firebase. As long as they defend the east, Perim Island in the Red Sea, and the west, this Gibraltar, all the power to control the Red Sea and the Mediterranean is in the hands of Britain, and not even one enemy ship will be able to enter or get out.

This day the wind was strong and the waves were very high. However it was a favorable wind and the ship was not shaky. Saw a lot of dolphins jumping around the ship. At 3:30 passed the narrowest part (about 4 miles) of the Strait of Gibraltar. Since we arrived in Portsaid on 11th, we have been on the Mediterranean for twelve days. Now the ship is going out into the Atlantic Ocean. The ship was directing northwest. The wind and waves were calm. At 6 p.m. to starboard saw the lighthouse of Cape Trafargar. There was nobody who didn't think of the time when Nelson was killed in the battle.

1月23日土曜　天気　Fair

Sunrise at 7:25. At 6 a.m. near to starboard saw Cape Vincent. The cape is located on hills ranging several miles end and there stands a temple where monks live. This temple is said to be the place where Nelson's dead body was laid at the Battle of Trafalgar.

From then on the ship gradually directed north. The position of the ship at noon: lat. 38°06' N and long. 9°26'W. The distance sailed since

ズボンは此河口にあり。

　1月24日日曜　天気　晴
　午前7時15分ポルチュガル国の山より日昇るを見る。正午船位、北緯42度58分、西経9度25分。前日正午より293哩。気暖波穏に恰も春の如し（55度）
　マルセーユ出帆以来地中海は波高く殊にヂブラルタル付近は一層波高く波高きを以て名高き大西洋は如何あらんと思い居りたるに返て波静に天気晴朗なり。印度及紅海にては終日1艘の船にも逢わざる事幾日もありたるに、さすが文明国の近海とて大西洋に出でてより通行の汽船帆船極て多く殊に今日は本船の前後左右に一時15艘の船を見たる時ありたり。午後1時スペーン国の西北端フィニステル港を右舷に見て過ぐ。是れより船は次第に東北の方向を取り。風波荒きを以て有名なるビスケー湾に入りたれども極て穏なり。日没4時45分。

　1月25日月曜　天気　晴
　日出7時21分。ビスケー湾も既に3分の2を過ぐ。此日も波穏なり。正午船位、北緯47度20分西経6度30分。前日正午より291哩。日没4時18分。午後6時半仏国西北角ブレスト灯台及ウーサンド（ousant）島灯台を右舷に見る。之れにて凡そ30時間を以て名高きビスケー湾も平穏に通過せり。

yesterday noon: 294 miles. At 2:30 p.m. saw Cape Roca, Portugal, near to starboard. To the southeast of this cape is a narrow bay and at the end of the bay is the Tagus estuary, where the capital Lisbon is located.

1月24日日曜　天気　Fair

At 7:15 saw the sunrise from the mountain in Portugal. The position of the ship at noon: lat. 42°58' N and long. 9°25' W. The distance sailed since yesterday noon: 293 miles. The climate was mild and the waves were calm as if in spring (55°).

Having had high waves since leaving Marseille, especially near Gibraltar, where the waves were even higher, I was wondering how the condition would be on the Atlantic, famous for its high waves, but unexpectedly we had calm waves and fine weather. Although while sailing on the Indian Sea and the Red Sea, we spent several days without seeing any ship all day, indeed we were now sailing coastal waters of civilized countries. Since we entered the Atlantic, we came across a lot of steamers and sailing ships, and today in particular, we found at one time fifteen ships around us. At 1 p.m. passed Port Finisterre, northwest end of Spain, to starboard. From here the ship gradually directed northeast. Entered the Bay of Biscay, notorious for its wild wind and waves, but it was very calm. Sunset at 4:45.

1月25日月曜　天気　Fair

Sunrise at 7:21. Already passed two thirds of Biscay Bay. The waves were calm today. The position of the ship at noon: lat. 7°20' N and long. 6°30' W. The distance sailed since yesterday noon: 291 miles. Sunset at 4:18. At 6:30 p.m. saw Breast Lighthouseat at the northwest corner of France and Island Ousant Lighthouse to starboard, which meant we safely passed the infamous bay in about 30 hours.

1月26日火曜　天気　晴

日出7時15分。午前11時ワイト島（Island of Wight）セントカセリーン（St. Catherine）岬を近く左舷に見る。本船は船名信号旗及会社旗を揚ぐ。此処はシグナルステーションなるを以て本船が何時何分通過したることをロンドン郵船会社支店に通知するなり。是より先き船尾の船名を改め煙突を元の通り黒に塗替え、空気大いに加わる。正午船位、北緯50度35分西経0度54分。前日正午より293哩。ロンドンまで175哩。午後7時ドーヴォル海峡を通過す。7時半右舷近くグードウィンサンド（Goodwin Sand）浅洲の灯台を見る。此日午後より薄霧あり。

1月27日水曜　天気　少雨　寒暖　暖

午前9時ロンドン市外アルボルトドック（Prince Albert Dock）着。郵船会社支店より石井君船迄来られ11時税関にて荷物の検査を受け、11時半の汽車にて（Custom House Station）石井君と同道。フェンチョルチスステーション（Fenchurch Station）迄行き夫れより郵船会社支店に至り三本君に面会。附近キャビンと云うレストーランにて昼食。A．B．C．（Aerated Bread Company）と云う処にてコーヒーを喫し再び支店に到り、5時過ぎ同氏と同道。ブロードストリートステーション（Broad Street Station）よりハムステッドステーション（Hampstead Heath Station）迄汽車に乗り6時頃スタンレーガーヅン44番（Stanley Gardens 44）ウォーコル氏（Mr. Walker）宅へ投宿す。

同宿には墺国留学生 Dr. Ritter 及仏国商人 M. Finnaly の2人あり。家族は夫婦に女子5人あり。下宿料は石炭洗濯の外1週参拾5志［注：志はシリングの意味］とす。（昼食及茶共）風呂は湯浴も冷水浴も随時に出来る。朝食9時頃、昼食1時半、茶5時頃、晩食（ヂンナル）7時半、日曜日は朝食9時半頃、昼食（ヂンナル）2時、晩食（サッパル）9時頃。

発信　日本自宅へ書状1

1月26日火曜　天気　Fair

Sunrise at 7:15. At 11 a.m. saw Island of Wight and Cape St. Catherine near to port. This ship hoisted the name flag, a signal flag and the company flag. This was a signal station to inform Yusen Kaisha London Branch when we passed it. From then on, the ship name at the stern was changed, the chimneys were repainted black and we were feeling excited. The position of the ship at noon: lat. 50°35' N and long. 0°54' W. The distance sailed since yesterday noon: 293 miles. 175 miles left to London. At 7 p.m. passed the Strait of Dover. Saw a lighthouse on Goodwin Sands near to starboard. This day had thin fog since the afternoon.

1月27日水曜　天気　Little rain　寒暖　Warm

At 9 a.m arrived at Prince Albert Dock outside London. Mr. Ishii from Yusen Kaisha London Branch came to the ship. At 11 a.m. had baggage inspected at the customs and at 11:30 a.m. with Mr. Ishii took a train at Custom House Station. Went as far as Fenchurch Station, then to Yusen Kaisha London Branch and met Mr. Mimoto. Had lunch at a nearby restaurant called Cabin. Had coffee at A.B.C. (Aerated Bread Company) and returned to the branch office. At 5 o'clock with him took a train from Broad Street Station to Hampstead Heath Station. Around 6 took a lodging at Mr. Walker, Stanley Gardens 44.

In this house are two other boarders: an Austrian student Dr. Ritter and a French merchant Mr. Finnaly. The family are a couple and five daughters. The fee is 35 shillings a week, excluding coal and laundry. Lunches and tea are included. A bath, both cold water and hot water, is available any time. Breakfast is served around 9 a.m., lunch 13:30 p.m., tea at around 5 p.m. and dinner at 7:30 p.m. On Sundays breakfast at around 9:30, dinner at 2 p.m. and supper at around 9 p.m.

受信　ロンドン郵船会社支店三本氏より書状1（テームズ河口グレーヴセンド停船中同地代理店より届来る。）

　　1月28日木曜　天気　少雨　寒暖　暖
　午前鈴木氏を訪ふ。種々当市の模様を聴く。氏は名古屋高等工業学校教授にして文部省留学生の工学士なり。
　午後四時半より鈴木氏同道。トテナムロード、ピカデリー、オックスフォールドストリート、リジェンドストリート等散歩見物。繁華眼を驚すばかりなり。薬種屋にてセメンタ求む。

　　1月29日金曜　天気　晴　寒暖　暖
　午前郵便局（Haverstock Hill）にて葉書を求め処々へ到着通知を認む。書籍屋よりベーデカルロンドン案内［注：当時ロンドンを訪れた日本人の多くが持っていた *Baedecker* という名の案内書］送り来る。
　午後鈴木氏を同町（スタンレーガーヅンス）51番に訪う。帰宅の際、居宅を間違い鈴を鳴らし戸を開かしめたるに見知らぬ女子出来りたれば粗こつを詫び居宅に帰り家人に語り大笑せり。
　4時半より鈴木君と同道。公使館に行き、林公使に面会談話少時。到達居りたる書状2封を受取り。オックスフォルトスツリート迄キャブにて来り夫れより鈴木君に別れバスにてアデレードタヴォルン迄来り下車して帰る。居宅付近にて路を失したれども路傍の人に尋ね帰宅す。

発信　米国シアトル服部氏へ葉書1
　　　伯林戸田氏へ葉書1
受信　自宅より1
　　　在伯林茨木氏より1

　　1月30日土曜　孝明天皇祭　天気　少雨
　三本君来訪。昼食を共にし家族と談話数時。鈴木氏を訪ふ。

1月28日木曜　天気　Little rain　寒暖　Warm

　Visited Mr. Suzuki in the morning. From him learned various things about this city. He is a professor at the Nagoya Techinical Institute, with a bachelor's of engineering, and sent by Ministry of Education.

　At 4:30 p.m. with him walked along Tottenham Road, Piccadilly, Oxford Street, Regent Street, and so on, looking at things. Quite surprised at the bustle of the streets. Bought cementa at a pharmacy.

1月29日金曜　天気　Fair　寒暖　Warm

　In the morning bought postcards at Haverstock Hill post office and wrote to several people to inform of my safe arrival here. Received Baedeker, a London guidebook, from a bookstore.

　In the afternoon visited Mr. Suzuki, at Stanley Gardens 51. On my way home when I rang a bell at a wrong house and the door opened, a girl I didn't know came out and I apologized for my rudeness. I told this to the people at my lodging and laughed a lot.

　At 4:30 p.m. visited Japanese legation with Mr. Suzuki. Talked with Minister Hayashi for some time. Received two letters from Japan there. Went to Oxford Street by cab and there parted with Mr. Suzuki and went to Adelaid Tavern by bus and while walking, got lost near the lodging, but by asking local people eventually managed to get home.

1月30日土曜　孝明天皇祭　天気　Little rain

　Mr. Mimoto called. Had lunch together and talked with the family for

発信　伯林茨木氏へ封書1

１月31日日曜　天気　少雨
午前11時ハヴォルストック（Haverstock St. Stephen）の会堂に行く。
午後鈴木氏来訪。共にプリムローズヒル及ハムステッドヒーズに散歩し、帰途茶を喫し帰宅す。

受信　東京帝国大学山崎直三氏より葉書1
　　　伯林戸田君より葉書1

２月

２月１日月曜　天気　少雨
午前 Dr. リットルと同道。ウェストミンストルアッペーを見物す。
チェーリングクロスの古本屋にて色々なる本を見る。［注；Charing Cross は古本屋街で有名である］午後１時半帰る。

２月２日火曜　天気　少雨
午前ドクトル・リットルと同道。ナショナルギャロリーに行き絵画を見る。*National Gallery Pictures* という本を買う（１志）。午後１時半帰る。
晩食前付近散歩す。食後日本行書状認む。

受信　文部省専門学務局長より通牒1

２月３日水曜　天気　少雨
午前午後日本行書状認む。三本氏より郵船発着表送来る。
晩食前付近散歩す。

発信　宅へ封書1　絵葉書1
　　　文部大臣へ到着届　封書1

a while. Visited Mr. Suzuki.

1月31日日曜　天気　Little rain

At 11 a.m went to the Hall of Haverstock St. Stephen.

In the afternoon Mr. Suzuki visited me. Took a walk together at Primrose Hill and Hampstead Heath, and on our way home had tea and returned home.

2月

2月1日月曜　天気　Little rain

In the morning with Dr. Ritter visited Westminster Abbey.

Looked at various books at the secondhand bookstores in Charing Cross. Returned at 1:30 p.m.

2月2日火曜　天気　Little rain

In the morning with Dr. Ritter visited National Gallery to see paintings. Bought a copy of National Gallery Pictures (one shilling). Returned home at 1:30 p.m.

Before dinner took a walk in the vicinity. After dinner wrote letters to send to Japan.

2月3日水曜　天気　Little rain

In the morning and in the afternoon wrote letters to send to Japan.

Received the Yusen ship's arrival & departure schedule from Mr. Mimoto.

Before dinner took a walk in the neighborhood.

　　　　北条氏へ封書1　三井物産宮本氏へ封書1
　　　　郵船会社本店荒井小林両氏連名　封書1
　　　　日本へ葉書6
　受信　宅より封書1
　　　　郵船会社支店三本氏より封書1

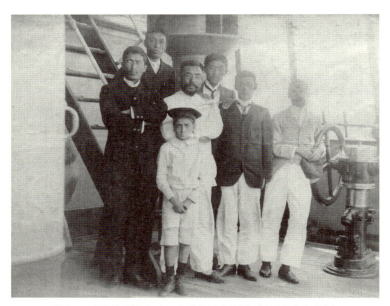

船中での撮影と思われる。右端が杉森此馬（柳川古文書館蔵）

ロンドン滞在日記

2月4日 - 9月21日

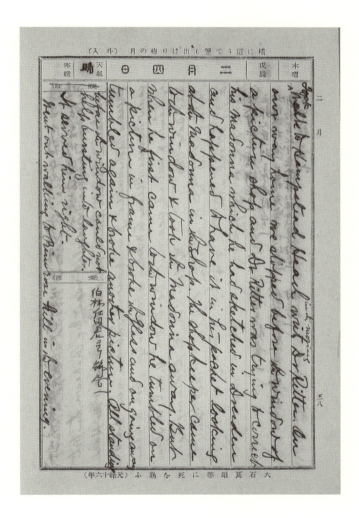

2月

2月4日木曜　天気　晴

Took walk to Hampstead Heath in the morning with Dr. Ritter. On our way home we stopped before the window of a picture shop and Dr. Ritter was trying to correct his Madonna which he had sketched in Dresden and happened to have it in his pocket looking at the Madonna in the shop. The shopkeeper came to the window & took the Madonna away. But when he first came to the window he tumbled on a picture in frame & broke the glass and on going away tumbled again & broke another picture. All standing before the window could not help bursting into laughter. It served him right. Went out walking to Primrose Hill in the evening.

受信　伯林戸田君より葉書1

2月5日金曜　天気　Fair

Went to the City & had an overcoat ordered at Chappell the tailor; Went to the Japanese consulet & saw Mr. Arakawa, then to the Yokohama Specie Bank & drew ￥100.00 & saw Mr. Hara, after seeing Messrs. Nishimaki, Yamakawa & Tatsumi went to the N. Y. K. & saw Messrs. Mimoto & Ishii to both of whom took a token of thanks & settled account. Went to the Y.M.C.A. Strand and saw Mr.[　] the secretary in the dining hall. Taking bus at the corner of Charing Cross came home at 7 1/2 o'clock p.m.

Went to bed at 12.

2月6日土曜　天気　Cloudy

Stayed at home almost all the day; took a short walk to Heath str.

2月

2月4日木曜　天気　晴

　午前ドクトル・リットルとハムステッド・ヒースまで散歩。帰宅途中、絵画店のウィンドウの前で立ち止まり、ドクトル・リットルはドレスデンでスケッチし、たまたまポケットに持っていたマドンナの絵を店のマドンナの絵を見ながら手直ししていた。店主がウィンドウのところにやってきて、マドンナの絵を持ち去ってしまった。しかし、まずウィンドウの所に来た時に額に入った絵につまずいてガラスを割ってしまい、去っていく時にもまた転んで別の絵を壊してしまった。ウィンドウの前に立っていた者たちは大笑いせずにはいられなかった。いい気味である。夕方はプリムローズ・ヒルに散歩に行った。

2月5日金曜　天気　晴

　シティに行って仕立て屋のチャペルでオーバーコートを注文した。日本領事館へ行き、アラカワ氏に会い、次に横浜正金銀行へ行き100円引き出し、ニシマキ氏、ヤマカワ氏、タツミ氏に会った後、ハラ氏に会った。NYK［注：日本郵船］に行き、三本氏とイシイ氏に会い、2人にお礼の品を持参し清算した。ストランドのYMCAへ行きダイニングホールの秘書［氏名不明］氏に会った。チャリングクロスの角からバスに乗り家に午後7時半に着いた。
　12時就寝。

2月6日土曜　天気　曇

　ほぼ終日家にいた。夕食前にヒースストリートに短い散歩に行き、夕食

before dinner & took walk again after dinner to Oxford Circus & had tea at the Frascati Restaurant which has a very large room that seemed to accommodate more than five hundred guests. There was a string band playing at every now & then.

発信　1 postcard to Mr. Hara Yokohama Specie Bank Bishop gate Str. Within.
受信　1 letter from Mr. Ibaraki Berlin.

2月7日日曜　天気　Fair

Met Mr. Chyujo at 51& went to the Congregational church, Lyndhurst Rd. to hear Dr. Horton.

Went again at 7 p.m. to hear Dr. Horton who spoke of the life of Mr. Gladstone. The church was quite full & the speaker was much applaused as he deserved.

2月8日月曜　天気　Cloudy

Learnt that the diplomatic negotiation between Japan & Russia was broken & the Japanese Minister in St. Petersburgh will leave for Berlin today & the formal declaration of war will be given today.

Played chess with Dr. Ritter.

Went to Chappell the tailor to try the overcoat on.

Went and saw the London Bridge, but it was on repair & could not see it very well.

Bought some pictorial postcards.

Learnt that the battle was opened from Japanese side and two Russian battle ships & one cruiser were tolpedoed and seriously damaged near Port Arthur and Japanese troops landed at Chemulpo taking two Russian steamers captive.

後はオックスフォード・サーカスまで歩き、フラスカティ・レストランでお茶を飲んだ。そこは500人もの客が入れそうな大きな部屋があった。時々弦楽器楽団が演奏した。

　2月7日日曜　天気　晴
　51番［注：鈴木氏宅］でチュウジョウ氏に会い、ホートン博士の話を聞きにリンドハースト・ロードの会衆派教会［注：キリスト教プロテスタントの一教派］へ行った。
　午後7時に再びホートン博士の話を聞きに行き、博士はグラッドストーンの人生について語られた。教会は満員で博士は大いに拍手を浴びており、それも当然のことである。

　2月8日月曜　天気　曇
　日本とロシアの外交交渉が決裂し、ペテスルブルグの日本大使は本日ベルリンへ発ち、宣戦布告が本日なされると知った。
　ドクトル・リットルとチェスをした。
　オーバーコートの試着に仕立て屋チャペルに行った。
　ロンドンブリッジを見に行ったが、修理中でよく見ることはできなかった。
　絵葉書を数枚買った。
　日本側から戦争が始り、2艘のロシア戦艦と巡洋艦1隻が旅順附近で魚雷により大きな損害を受けた。日本軍は仁川に上陸し2隻のロシアの気船を確保したということがわかった。
　［注：日露戦争は1904年（明治37年）2月8日に開戦、1905年9月5日に終結。陸上戦は満州南部、遼東半島が主な戦場、海上は日本近海での艦

受信　A postal from Mr. Hara

　２月９日火曜　天気　Rainy

　　Went to National Gallery after breakfast and came back at 1 1/2 o'clock.

　　Wrote letters in the afternoon.

　　Bought a catalogue of the National Gallery.

　　Bought *Stories from Browning* (2/-).

　　Learned further particulars of Japan's first victory & bombardment of Port Arthur.

　２月10日水曜　天気　Fair Rainy after

　　Took a walk as far as Euston & back.

　　Saw on play card ［注：placard か］　six Russian ships were damaged 7 killed & 56 wounded.

発信　A letter to Mr. Bekki.

　　　A letter to Mr. Shimidzu.

　　　Two postals to home.

　　　A postal to the students of the Hiroshima H. N. C. ［注：Hiroshima Normal College 広島高等師範学校のこと］

　２月11日木曜　紀元節　天気　Fair

　　Went to the British Museum & saw many valuable collections. Bought *the complete works of Shakespeare* (2/-).

　　Often greeted by strangers in the street for Japan's good opening.

　　Went out walking to Hampstead Heath.

受信　1 Parcel sent from Chappell.

　　　A letter from home.

隊戦が繰り広げられた]

2月9日火曜　天気　雨
朝食後ナショナル・ギャラリーに行って、午後1時半帰宅。
午後は書状を認めた。
ナショナル・ギャラリーのカタログを購入。
ブラウニングの物語を購入（2シリング）。
旅順における日本の初勝利と爆撃の詳細がさらにわかった。

2月10日水曜　天気　晴後雨
ユーストンまで歩き、また戻ってきた。
プラカードに6隻のロシア船がやられ、7名死亡、56名負傷と書いてあった。

その日の重大事件を印刷したプラカードを見せながら夕刊を売るニュースボーイ（伊地知純正著、『倫敦名所図会』研究社、1918刊より）

2月11日木曜　紀元節　天気　晴
大英博物館へ行き、多くの貴重な収集品を見た。シェイクスピア全集を2シリングで買った。
街で見知らぬ人から日本の勝利について何度も言葉をかけられる。
ハムステッド・ヒースに散歩に出かけた。

2月12日金曜　天気　Rainy

Went out walking to Primrose Hill in the morning.

After lunch went out intending to go to St. Andrews str., but finding it too windy & wet came back from Haverstock Hill & stayed at home all the afternoon & evening.

2月13日土曜　天気　Fair Windy

Took bath in the morning. In the afternoon went to St. Andrews str. & tried to find out St. Andrews University to see Dr. Bosanquet, but two or three passers by nor policemen there could tell where it is. On inquiry at the post office I was told that it is in Scotland! Stupid enough. Then went to Exeter Hall where Japanese Christians in London had a monthly meeting; was happy to meet with Dr.Whitney who is going back to Japan in a few weeks. Made a short address on the 23rd Psalm.

発信　A letter to Miss Snowdon.

2月14日日曜　天気　Cloudy windy

Got up late. Went to Congregational Church to hear Dr. Horton who preached our "except a man be born of water and of the Spirit, he cannot enter into the kingdom of God"(St. John. 3:5)

Went to the Congregational Church in the evening to hear Dr. Horton once more. He spoke on why Christians are not better men than those who are not Christian.

Played chess after supper － drawn game.

2月15日月曜　天気　Cloudy

Spent whole morning in reading.

No fresh war news in morning paper.

Another Russian cruiser sinks. – placard (evening).

2月12日金曜　天気　雨
　午前中プリムローズ・ヒルに散歩にでかけた。
　昼食後セントアンドリュース・ストリートまで行こうと出かけたが、風雨がとても強く、ハーバーストックヒルから帰って来て、午後と夕方はずっと家にいた。

2月13日土曜　天気　晴風強し
　朝入浴。午後はセントアンドリュース通りに行って、ボサンケット博士に会うためにセントアンドリュース大学に行こうとしたが、2、3名の通行人もそこにいた警官もどこにあるか知らなかった。郵便局で尋ねてみて、それはスコットランドにあると言われたのだ！　何という失態だ。それから、ロンドン在住の日本人のキリスト教徒が毎月集まっているエクセターホールに行った。ホイットニー博士に会えてうれしく思った。ホイットニー博士は2、3週間後に日本に戻る予定である。詩編23編について少し話した。

2月14日日曜　天気　曇風強し
　朝遅く起きた。会衆派教会へホートン博士の説教を聞きに行った。彼はヨハネによる福音書3章5節の、「もしも水と御霊から生まれなければ、人は神様の御国に入ることはできません」について説いた。
　夜もう一度ホートン博士の説教を聞きに会衆派教会へ行った。彼はキリスト教徒でない人たち以上に、なぜキリスト教徒が善良とは言えないのかを語った。
　夕食後はチェスをした。引き分けに終わった。

2月15日月曜　天気　曇
　午前中ずっと読書。
　朝刊には新しい戦争のニュースはない。
　またロシアの巡洋艦が沈没。プラカード（夕方）。

発信　1 postal to Mr. Omiya (Newcastle-on-Tyne).
　　　A letter to Miss Burnside.
受信　A letter to C. L. Burnside.

2月16日火曜　天気　Cloudy

Wrote letters in the morning. Went in the afternoon to see Mr. Doi at Gower Str. but was disappointed not to find him at home.

Saw Mr. Doi at Mr. Suzuki's where Mr. Doi paid a visit late in the afternoon. Had a pleasant visit from Messrs. Doi & Suzuki in the evening & chatted till midnight.

受信　A letter from Miss Snowdon.

2月17日水曜　天気　Snow

Wrote letters in the morning. Saw first snow in London. Went to see Miss Burnside at George Lane (Woodford) in the afternoon and spent a very pleasant time.

Reported another Russian warship torpedoed.

発信　A letter to Miss Snowdon.

2月18日木曜　天気　Fair

Wrote letters in the morning & afternoon. Went to the Drury Lane with Messrs. Doi, Suzuki & Hirayama in the evening. It was extremely beautiful & baffles description altogether. The scene was sometimes the depicts of forests & at other time the bottom of the sea. How sea weeds grew & fish swam were just wonderful. Fish were magnified shadows of real fish I should think. How the spirits of pearls swam in supported mid-water was wonderful entirely.

Came back rather late.

2月16日火曜　天気　曇
　午前中手紙を認めた。午後は土井氏をガワーストリートに尋ねたが、残念ながら不在だった。
　土井氏が午後鈴木氏のところを訪問しており、そこで土井氏に会った。夜に両氏が私を訪ねてくれて、夜中まで楽しく話が弾んだ。

2月17日水曜　天気　雪
　午前中は手紙を認めた。ロンドンで初めての雪を見た。午後はジョージレーン（ウッドフォード）にバーンサイド嬢に会いに行き、とても楽しく過ごした。
　またロシアの戦艦が魚雷で沈没したことが報じられた。

2月18日木曜　天気　晴
　午前と午後手紙を認めた。夕方は土井氏、鈴木氏、平山氏とドルリー・レーン劇場に行った。極めて美しく筆舌に尽くしがたい描写であった。舞台の背景は森の時もあり海の底の時もある。海藻が生え魚が泳ぐ様子は実に素晴らしかった。魚は本当の魚の拡大された影のように思われた。真珠の精が水中のイメージの中を泳ぐ姿がまことにすばらしかった。
　かなり遅く帰宅した。

受信　A letter from home (1/17(?)).
　　　The Student.

2月19日金曜　天気　Very　fine　寒暖　Icy

Went to Putney to see Miss Snowdon at her father's house & spending very pleasant hours. Came home late in the afternoon. Took train from Swiss Cottage station on going & "bus" on returning.

受信　Pt. Card from Mr. Doi.
　　　The Student (Xmas number).

2月20日土曜　天気　Cloudy　寒暖　Warm

Wrote letters and postals in the morning. Took lunch at Exeter Hall & went to see Miss Pope at Swanley, Kent. Became a member of the International Club under Miss Pope. Each member is to write a composition on the subject given once a month. Miss Pope corrects the papers which are circulated among the members. Among the members are some German ladies French Irish Japanese & English gentlemen. The next meeting is to be held on the 25 □□□ The subject for this month is "Woman's Position in the World." Came home late in the evening.

発信　A letter to Kobayashi & letters & ptcards to friends in Japan.
　　　A letter to the Department of Education, Tokyo.

2月21日日曜　天気　Cloudy　寒暖　Warm

Went to St. Paul's Cathedral. This is the largest church in London. Went to Dr. Horton's church in the evening.

2月19日金曜　天気　快晴　寒暖　極寒
　プットニーに行き、スノードン嬢を父上の家に訪ね、楽しい時を過ごした。午後遅く帰宅した。行きはスイスコテッジ駅から列車に乗り、帰りは「バス」に乗った。

2月20日土曜　天気　曇　寒暖　暖
　午前中は手紙や葉書を認めた。エクセターホールで昼食を食べ、ポープ嬢をケントのスワンリーに訪ねた。ポープ嬢が主催する国際クラブの会員になった。各会員が月1回与えられたテーマで英作文をすることになっている。ポープ嬢が添削したペーパーが会員の間で回覧される。会員の中には、数人のドイツ人婦人にフランス人、アイルランド人、日本人、イギリス人の男性がいる。次の会合は25□□□に開催されることになっている。今月のテーマは「世界における女性の地位」である。夜遅く帰宅。

2月21日日曜　天気　曇　寒暖　暖
　セントポール寺院に行った。ロンドン最大の教会である。
　夜はホートン博士の教会に行った。

2月22日月曜

　Went to Oxford with Doi, Soga, & Suzuki. Mr. Hirata came to meet us at the Station.

　Saw different Colleges --Christ Church where Gladstone was educated, Pembroke where Johnson was educated, &c &c. Went to see College Boat race at the Cherwell River. New College is a very old building and the wall is said to be remains of Romans(?). Johnson's Walk is a nice avenue which Johnson used to take walk it is said. In the evening went to a theater, the play was "Resurrection." Took pictures in group. Stayed overnight at a boarding house.

発信　A postal to home.
　　　Postals to friends (From Oxford).
　　　A letter to Mr. Burnside.
受信　A letter from Mr. Burnside.

2月23日火曜

　Saw different places in Oxford. Came back late in the evening; had dinner at the Frascati Restaurant, Oxford str.

2月24日水曜　天気　Cloudy　寒暖　Cold

　Spent the whole morning in writing composition (Woman's Position in the World), and letters. Went to see Mr. Doi & went together to the Army & Navy Store bought some envelopes & notepapers. Went to the His Majesty where we saw a Japanese play "A Darling of God." Nothing is so ridiculous, nothing is so nonsentical. Everything in Japan put together in a perfect per mer (ママ). Scenes are very nice.

発信　A letter to Miss Pope.
　　　A postal to Mr. Hara.

2月22日月曜
　オックスフォードに土井氏、ソガ氏、鈴木氏と出かけた。平田氏が駅に迎えに来てくれた。いろんなカレッジを見た。
　グラッドストーンが学んだクライストチャーチやジョンソンが学んだペングローブなどなど。チャーウェル川での大学のボートレースを見物。ニューカレッジは大変古い建物で壁はローマ時代（？）の遺構とのこと。ジョンソンズウォークはジョンソンが散歩した美しい通りと言われている。夜は劇場に行って、芝居は「復活」であった。皆で写真を撮った。下宿屋に一泊した。

2月23日火曜
　オックスフォードのいろいろな場所を見学した。夜遅く帰宅し、オックスフォードストリートのフレスカティ・レストランで夕食をとった。

2月24日水曜　天気　曇　寒暖　寒
　午前中はずっと英作文（世界における女性の地位）と書状を書いた。土井氏を訪ね、一緒に陸軍海軍ストアに行き封筒やメモ用紙を購入。ヒズマジェスティ劇場に行って日本の芝居「神々の寵児」を鑑賞。これほど馬鹿げたものはない、これほどナンセンスなものはない。日本のいろんなものがいっしょくたになって完璧なものになっている。舞台装置は素晴らしかった。
　［注：「神々の寵児」David Belasco と John Luther Long によるジャポニズム演劇で牧野義男が舞台装置・衣装・メイクアップを担当、好評を博した］

２月25日木曜　天気　Snowy　寒暖　Cold
　　Had hair cut; took bath in the morning.

発信　A letter to Dr. Whitney
　　　Postals to Toda, Berlin; Nakanome, Wien; Ikeda, Tokyo.
　　　Newspapers to Mr. Hojo, Hiroshima.
受信　A letter from Mr. Hara.
　　　A postal from Herr Toda from Berlin.
　　　Another letter from Mr. Hara.

２月26日金曜　天気　Little Snow　寒暖　Cold
　　Spent the morning in reading & a short walk.

２月27日土曜　天気　Fair　寒暖　Cold
　　Spent the morning in reading & writing. Went to see Dr. Whitney at the Nikko Lodge at Harlesden in the afternoon & came home about eight o'clock in the evening.

２月28日日曜　天気　Fair Snow after　寒暖　Very Cold
　　In the morning went to the Oratory a ［注：at か］ Catholic Church & taking lunch in a restaurant where saw six Japanese gentlemen, went to the Kensington Museum then to the Albert Hall to hear the music. On coming out of the Hall found snowing & it was very nice in the Hyde Park by which we (Doi, Suzuki & myself) rode on the bus but it was very cold to ride on the top. Then went to Mr. Mason's 52 Gower st. Mr. Doi's lodging where we took tea & saw 2 military officers & 1 naval officer who are going back to Japan in a few days. Came home at 9 o'clock.

２月29日月曜
　　Spent all the day in reading and writing taking a short walk late in

2月25日木曜　天気　雪　寒暖　寒
午前中散髪と入浴。

2月26日金曜　天気　小雪　寒暖　寒
午前中読書と少し散歩。

2月27日土曜　天気　晴　寒暖　寒
午前中読書と英作文。午後はハーレスデンのNikkoロッジにホイットニー博士を訪ね、夜8時頃帰宅。

2月28日日曜　天気　晴後雪　寒暖　非常に寒い
午前カトリック教会のオラトリに行った。レストランで昼食を取っているとき、6人の日本人の紳士にあった。ケンジントン博物館へ行き、次には音楽を聴きにアルバートホールに行った。ホールから出てくると雪が降っていて、ハイドパークはきれいだった。そこから我々（土井氏、鈴木氏、私）はバスに乗った。しかし2階に乗るのはとても寒かった。それから土井氏が下宿しているガワーストリート52番のメイソン氏宅に行き、お茶を飲み、2人の軍人と1人の海軍士官に会った。彼等は数日中に日本に帰るそうだ。9時に帰宅した。

2月29日月曜
1日中読書と英作文、午後遅く少し散歩。

the afternoon.

発信　A postal to Mr. Hirata (Oxford).
　　　Postals to friends, Japan.

3月

3月1日火曜　天気　Snow　寒暖　Cold

Spent the whole morning in writing letters.
went to the Harlot (?) Stove (a very large bazaar) then to see Mr. Soga at the Crescent Hotel & dropping in at 82 Gower Str. to take warmth & came home late in the evening. Very cold. Messrs. Doi& Suzuki were in company all the afternoon & evening.

3月2日水曜　天気　Snow little Rain　寒暖　Cold

Wrote letters in the morning.

発信　A letter to home.
　　　Postals to friends, Japan.
受信　Mr. Hirata, Oxford.
　　　Mr. Nakanome, Wien.

3月3日木曜　天気　Rain & Snow after

Spent the whole morning in reading.
　Went to the International College & two other schools of Languages & made inquiry, but found them unsatisfactory.

発信　A postal to Kobayashi, Tokyo.
　　　A postal o Nakayama, Sendai.
受信　A postal from Mr. Ibaraki

3月

　3月1日火曜　天気　雪　寒暖　寒
　午前中ずっと書状を認めた。
　ハーロット・ストーブ（とても大きな市場）に行き、それからクレッセント・ホテルのソガ氏に会いに行った。体を温めにガワーストリート82番［注：土井氏下宿］に立ち寄り、夜遅く帰宅した。とても寒い。土井氏と鈴木氏と午後と夜中ずっと一緒だった。

　3月2日水曜　天気　雪小雨　寒暖　寒
　朝、手紙を認めた。

　3月3日木曜　天気　雨後雪
　午前中はずっと読書をして過ごした。
　インターナショナルカレッジと2つの語学学校に行き、問い合わせをしたが、満足いくものではなかった。

3月4日金曜　天気　Cloudy　寒暖　Cold

Spent the morning in reading. In the afternoon went to see Mr. Gomsersall at his residence & made inquiry of taking a private lesson. He charges a ginea for 6 lessons.

Went to see Mr. Doi & with Mr. Suzuki went to a Turkish bath & came back late in the evening. The Turkish bath is not an ordinary bath, it has three or four apartments of different degrees of warmth. 1st R.is of 160°Fh. 2nd 180°, 3rd 260°(?) and it is said to be 250°.We sit in chair in these warm rooms beginning from the lowest in degree & changing rooms to the highest. We get perspired very much & afterward have ourselves washed in other apartment.

発信　A postal to Mr. Ibaraki.

3月5日土曜　天気　Cloudy

Had a visit from Mr. Ibaraki who had returned from Berlin two days ago. He stayed & took lunch with us. Went to Snaresbrook to see Mr. Burnside & came back at 7 1/2.

Spent the early part of the morning in reading Shakespeare; with Dr. Ritter.

3月6日日曜　天気　Cloudy　寒暖　Cold

Spent the morning in reading Shakespeare; *Twelfth Night* with Dr. Ritter. Went to see Mr. Doi & found Mr. Kumamoto there & also met Mr. Shiba sent by the Nippon Tetsudo Kaisha. Went to the Jiyutei to take Japanese supper & again went to Mrs. Mason's, and had a conversation with an American girl about the education in America.

3月7日月曜

Spent the morning & evening in reading Shakespeare.

3月4日金曜　天気　曇　寒暖　寒
　午前中は読書をして過ごした。午後はゴマサール氏を邸宅に訪ね、個人レッスンが受けられるか問い合わせた。6回の授業に対して1ギニー払う。
　土井氏を訪ね、鈴木氏と一緒にトルコ風呂に行き、夜遅く帰宅した。トルコ風呂というのは普通の風呂ではなくて、三つか四つの温度が異なる区分に分かれている。一つ目は華氏160度で、二つ目は180度、三つ目は260度（？）、250度と言われる。温かい部屋で椅子に座りながら、温度が低い部屋から最も高い部屋へと部屋を変えていった。大いに発汗し、その後別の部屋で体を洗ってもらう。

3月5日土曜　天気　曇
　2日前にベルリンから帰ってきた茨木［注：清次郎］氏が訪ねてきた。彼は滞在し昼食をともにした。バーンサイド氏に会うためにスネアスブルックに行き、7時半に帰宅した。
　午前の早い時間はシェイクスピアの『十二夜』をドクトル・リットルと共に読んだ。

3月6日日曜　天気　曇　寒暖　寒
　午前中はドクトル・リットルとシェイクスピアの『十二夜』を読んだ。土井氏に会いに行くとそこに隈本［注：有尚］氏がいて、また日本鉄道会社から派遣されたシバ氏にも会った。自由亭に日本食を食べに行き、またメイソン夫人宅へ行って、アメリカ人の女の子とアメリカの教育について会話した。

3月7日月曜
　午前中と夜シェイクスピアを読んで過ごした。

Wrote letters & postals.

受信　A postal from Mr. R. Kodama, Newcastle-on-Tyne.

3月8日火曜　天気　Fair　寒暖　Warm p.m. 56°
Spent the morning & evening in reading Shakespeare & others.
Went to Mr. Gomersall & took lesson, read newspaper & had some letters corrected. Paid £ 1/1/0 for 6 lessons.

3月9日水曜　天気 Fair　寒暖　Warm 40°–60°
Spent the whole morning in reading. Took bath at 12. Took walk to Hampstead Heath. Spent the evening in reading.

発信　A letter to home.
　　　Postals to Mr. Kodama, Newcastle & friends in Japan.
　　　A letter to Mr. Burnside.
受信　A letter from Mr. Burnsie.

3月10日木曜　天気　Fair　寒暖　39°-47°
Read Shakespeare in the morning & evening. Went to see Mr. Ibaraki at Walterton Rd.

3月11日金曜　天気　Fair
Spent the morning & evening in reading. Finished *Love's Labour's Lost*.
Went to Mr. Gomersall's to take lesson.

受信　A postal from Mr. Hara.

手紙と葉書を認めた。

3月8日火曜　天気　晴　寒暖　暖午後56°
　午前中と夜はシェイクスピアや他の本を読んで過ごした。
　ゴマサール氏の所に行ってレッスンを受け、新聞を読み手紙を数通訂正してもらった。6回のレッスン代として1ポンド1シリング払った。

3月9日水曜　天気　晴　寒暖　暖40°－60°
　午前中はずっと本を読んだ。12時に入浴した。ハムステッド・ヒースまで散歩に行った。夜も読書をした。

3月10日木曜　天気　晴　寒暖　39°－47°
　午前中と夜シェイクスピアを読んだ。ウォルタートンロードに茨木氏を訪ねた。

3月11日金曜　天気　晴
　午前中と夜読書をした。『恋の骨折り損』を読み終えた。
　ゴマサール氏のところにレッスンを受けに行った。

3月12日土曜　天気　Foggy fair after

Began to read *Macbeth* & spent the greater part of the morning on that.

Went to Exeter Hall in the afternoon & had the first from Mr. Burnside. Held the monthly meeting in the same place afterward. 6 Japanese Xians & 4 foreigners & 3 children assembled in the meeting.

3月13日日曜　天気　Fair　寒暖　38°－48°

Read Shakespeare in the morning & went to the Congregational church, Lyndhurst Road.

発信　A letter to Mr. Kachi, Mitsui & Co.

3月14日月曜　天気　Fair　寒暖　38°－48°

Spent the whole morning in reading Shakespeare. Took walk to Primrose Hill. Wrote letters and read Shakespeare in the afternoon and evening. Enjoying a fair weather every day. Conscious of near approach of Spring.

3月15日火曜　天気　Very fair　寒暖　44°－48°

Spent the morning in reading Shakespeare & made some preparation to go to Mr. Gomersall's where I went in the afternoon to take usual lesson.

Read Shakespeare in the evening.

発信　A letter & postals to home.
受信　A letter from Mr. Kachi.

3月16日水曜　天気　Fair　寒暖　45°－50°

Spent the morning in reading & writing letters. After lunch went to

3月12日土曜　天気　霧後晴

『マクベス』を読み始め、午前中の大部分は『マクベス』に費やした。午後エクセタホールに行って、バーンサイド氏の1回目があった。後で月例会が同じ場所であった。集会には6名の日本人キリスト教徒と外国人4名、子供3名が集まった。

3月13日日曜　天気　晴　寒暖　38°- 48°

午前中はシェイクスピアを読み、リンドハースト・ロードの会衆派教会に行った。

3月14日月曜　天気　晴　寒暖　38°- 48°

午前中ずっとシェイクスピアを読んで過ごした。プリムローズ・ヒルに散歩に行った。午後と夜は手紙を書いてシェイクスピアを読んだ。毎日好天に恵まれている。春が近づいていることを感じる。

3月15日火曜　天気　快晴　寒暖　44°- 48°

午前中はシェイクスピアを読み、ゴマサール氏宅へ行く準備をし、午後はゴマサール氏宅で平常のレッスンを受けた。

夜はシェイクスピアを読んだ。

3月16日水曜　天気　晴　寒暖　45°- 50°

午前中は読書と手紙を書いて過ごした。昼食後日本公使館へ行って、テ

the Japanese Legation & took walk to the other side of the Thames crossing Lambert Bridge on going & Westminster Bridge on coming back.

　　Read Shakespeare in the evening.

発信　A letter to Miss Bosanquet, Japan.
受信　A letter from Miss Snowdon.

3月17日木曜　天気　Fair

　　Spent morning in reading, writing letters. Took bath at noon. Went to see Miss Waber at Randolph Rd. Maida Hill, took a long time to find out the right place. Mean to go to him to take lesson from next month. Glad to get a letter from home after a long silence.

　　Went to hear Mr. Gomersall's lecture on Shelly in the Haverstock Presbyterian Church. Saw there Dr. Gasuet one of the greatest living authorities of Shelly.

発信　Letters to Miss Snowdon; to Miss Waber; to Dr. Whitney; to Mr. Lloyd; to Mr. Beacon.
受信　Letters from Seki, Hiroshima; from Miss Waber,; from Dr. Whitney; from Mr. Beacon.
　　Letter from home.

3月18日土曜　天気　Fair

　　Read Shakespeare in the morning & evening. Went to Mr. Gomersall's to take usual lesson. Sang after tea & a short time after dinner. Went to Haverstock Post Office & made an inquiry of the location of Brandiston Rd. St Peter's Park & learned that it is in the back of Maida Vale.

発信　A postal to Mr. Ibaraki.

ムズ川の対岸へ散歩し、行きはランバート橋を渡り、帰りはウエストミンスター橋を渡って帰って来た。
　夜はシェイクスピアを読んだ。

　　3月17日木曜　天気　晴
　午前中は読書と手紙を書いて過した。昼に入浴。メイダヒルのランドルフロードのウェイバー嬢の所に行ったが、場所を見つけるのに長い時間がかかった。来月からレッスンを受けるつもりだ。自宅からしばらくぶりに手紙が来てうれしく思った。
　ハーバーストック長老教会にシェリーに関するゴマサール氏の講演を聞きに行った。そこで存命のシェリー研究の大家の1人ガスケ博士に会った。

　　3月18日土曜　天気　晴
　午前と夜にシェイクスピアを読んだ。いつものレッスンを受けにゴマサール氏宅へ行った。お茶の後、夕食の直後に歌を歌った。ハーバーストック郵便局に行ってセントピーターズパークのブランディストン・ロードの場所を尋ね、メイダベイルの裏にあることがわかった。

受信　A postal from Mr. Ibaraki.

3月19日月曜　天気　Rain

Read Shakespeare in the morning & evening.
Went to see Mr. Lloyd at Brandiston Rd.
Mr. Burnside came to give lesson.
Messrs. Kachi & Kawabe called.

受信　A letter from Mr. Ibaraki.

3月20日月曜　天気　Cloudy　寒暖　Warm

Read Shakespeare (*Caesar*) in the morning & evening.
Dr. Uchida called. Mr. Mimoto called.
Went to see Mr. Deacon, X Chruch Vicarage Cannon place, near Hampstead Heath.
Went to see Mr. Doi in the evening.

3月21日月曜　天気　Rain

Read Shakespeare in the early part of morning. Went to Euston Station to see Mr. Doi off. Went to see the school where Mr. Lloyd teaches woodwork. Saw the Woodwork Room, Chemistry Room Geography & Grammar classes.

Mr. Yamazaki from Oxford came to stay a week or so.

3月22日火曜　天気　Fair

Read Shakespeare (*Hamlet*) in the morning. Went to see the funeral procession of late Duke of Cambridge to Westbourne□□□. The King was the chief mourner.

Took lunch in a restaurant in Edgware Rd. & came home at 3 p.m.
Went to take lesson. Read Shakespeare in the evening.

3月19日月曜　天気　雨
午前と夜にシェイクスピアを読んだ。
ブランディストン・ロードにロイド氏を訪ねた。
バーンサイド氏がレッスンをしに来てくれた。
加地氏とカワベ氏が訪ねてきた。

3月20日月曜　天気　曇　寒暖　暖
午前と夜にシェイクスピア（『シーザー』）を読んだ。
内田［注：銀蔵］博士が訪ねてきた。三本氏が訪ねてきた。
ハムステッド・ヒースの近くのキャノンプレイスのキリスト教会牧師館にディーコン氏に会いにいった。
夜は土井氏に会いに行った。

3月21日月曜　天気　雨
午前の早い時間はシェイクスピアを読んだ。ユーストン駅に土井氏を見送りに行った。ロイド氏が木工を教えている学校を見学に行った。木工室、化学室、地理と文法の授業を見学した。
オックスフォードの山崎［注：宗直］氏がやって来て1週間程度滞在することになった。

3月22日火曜　天気　晴
午前中はシェイクスピア（『ハムレット』）を読んだ。故ケンブリッジ侯爵の葬列を見ようとウェストボーン□□□に行った。国王が喪主だった。
エッジウェア・ロードのレストランで昼食を取り、午後3時に帰宅した。
レッスンを受けに行った。夜はシェイクスピアを読んだ。

ロンドン滞在日記　77

受信　A postal from Mr. Doi, Manchester.
　　　A postal from Miss D. Pope, Secretary of the International Club.

3月23日水曜

Read Shakespeare in the morning & afternoon. Wrote letters. Went to hear Shakespearian manuscript in Royal Society of Literature at the Medical Hall in Hanover Square in the evening.

発信　A letter to Miss D. Pope.
受信　A postal from Mr. S. Kato, Newcastle-on-Tyne.

3月24日木曜　天気　Fair

Read Shakespeare in the morning. Wrote letters.

Went to Yokohama Specie Bank to receive money ¥150.00 (£ 14-18-5), then to Chappell, the tailor, Graham str. to order a mourning coat (£ 2-17-6).

Went to Camden Theater to see "Macbeth" played by Mr. & Mrs. Benson.

発信　Letter to home, Mr. Hojo, Mr. Seki.
　　　Postals to home & Mr. T. Tanaka, Etajima; Mr. S. Kato, Newcastle-on-Tyne.

3月25日金曜　天気　Cloudy　寒暖　Cold

Read Shakespeare in the morning & evening. Went to take lesson in the afternoon.

発信　To Mr. Burnside.
受信　From Mr. Doi, on board the Ship of White Star Liner at Queen's Town.

3月23日水曜

　午前と夜にシェイクスピアを読んだ。書状を認めた。夜はハノーバー・スクエアのメディカルホールで行われた王立文学協会にシェイクスピアの手書き原稿の話を聞きに行った。

3月24日木曜　天気　晴

　午前中シェイクスピアを読んだ。書状を認めた。
　横浜正金銀行に150円（14ポンド18シリング5ペンス）を受け取りに行った。それからグレイシャム・ストリートの仕立屋のチャペルにモーニング・コートを注文しに行った（2ポンド17シリング6ペンス）。
　カムデン劇場にベンソン夫妻が演じる「マクベス」を観に行った。

3月25日金曜　天気　曇　寒暖　寒

　午前と夜はシェイクスピアを読んだ。午後はレッスンを受けに行った。

3月26日土曜　天気　Cloudy

Read Shakespeare in the morning. Went to Camden Theater to see the play of Julius Caesar in the afternoon & Hamlet in the evening.

Oxford & Cambridge boat race took place in Putney; Cambridge won.

受信　Postals from Mr. Ibaraki & from Mr. Burnside.
　　　Compos in package.

3月27日日曜　天気　Fairr

Read Shakespeare (*Tempest*) in the morning.
Took a walk to Hampstead Heath.
Read Shakespeare in the evening.

3月28日月曜

Read Shakespeare in the morning & evening.

Went to the City to fit the coat in Chappell's. Went to Yokohama Specie Bank & handed compositions to Mr. Hara.

発信　A letter to Mr. Shattack.
受信　A letter from Mr. Shattack.
　　　A book (David Copperfield) from Mr. Ibaraki.

3月29日火曜　天気　Cloudy rain　寒暖　Warm

Shakespeare reading in the morning. In the afternoon went out walking & had visiting card ordered in Chalk Farm Road. Bought 2 teacloths in Haverstock Hill. Thunder storm in the afternoon. Read Shakespeare before dinner. Had a visit from Mr. Ibaraki stayed till 11.

受信　A letter from Dr. Whitney enclosing a note of introduction to Dr. Horton.

3月26日土曜　天気　曇

　午前中はシェイクスピアを読んだ。カムデン劇場に午後は「ジュリアス・シーザー」を、夜は「ハムレット」を見に行った。

　オックスフォードとケンブリッジのボートレースがプットニーで開催された。ケンブリッジが勝った。

3月27日日曜　天気　晴

　午前中シェイクスピア（『テンペスト』）を読んだ。

　ハムステッド・ヒースに散歩に行った。

　夜シェイクスピアを読んだ。

3月28日月曜

　午前と夜にシェイクスピアを読んだ。

　チャペルでコートを試着するためにシティに行った。横浜正金銀行に行って英作文をハラ氏に渡した。

3月29日火曜　天気　曇雨　寒暖　暖

　午前中はシェイクスピアを読んだ。午後は散歩に出かけて、チョーク・ファーム・ロードで名刺を注文した。ハーバーストックヒルで茶巾を2枚買った。午後は雷雨。夕食前シェイクスピアを読んだ。茨木氏が訪ねてきて11時迄滞在した。

Postals from Mr. Shattack & Mr. Yamazaki, Oxford.

3月30日水曜　天気　Fair aft: Snow & rain　寒暖　Cold.
Read Shakespeare in the morning & wrote letters.

Visiting card done. Went to see Mr. Shattach in the afternoon. Played Chess in the evening.

Read *David Copperfield* a little.

First land fight on Korean land was reported resulting in the victory to the Japanese. The Russians stationed at Chonju were obliged to evacuate their station & the Japanese entered the town in triumph.

発信　A postal to Mr. Shattack.

3月31日木曜　天気　Cloudy
Read Shakespeare in the morning & evening. Received a parcel from Chappell, finding the coat too tight, took it again to Chappell in the afternoon. Read *Davy*.

On coming back from the City taking a wrong way asked the policeman several times to go to the Strand & at last taking a bus near Old str. went to Tottenham Court Rd., then walking to Euston, took a bus again to Adelaide & walked home; happened to meet Mr. Suzuki in the bus at Euston.

4月

4月1日金曜　天気　Fair
Read Shakespeare in the morning & evening. Went to see Dr. Whitney at Camden Rd. introduced to his father-in-law Mr. Braithwart who showed Greek M. N. S. of New Testament & read Isaiah 3 chap. in Hebrew. Took tea there. Shops shut (Good Friday). Saw many going to

3月30日水曜　天気　晴　午後雪雨　寒暖　寒

午前中シェイクスピアを読み、書状を認めた。

名刺ができた。午後シャタック氏を訪ねた。夜チェスをした。

『デイビッド・カッパーフィールド』を少し読んだ。

朝鮮における初の陸上戦は日本の勝利に終わったと報じられている。全州に駐屯したロシア軍は駐屯地を退去せざるを得ず、日本軍が大勝利の中街に入った。

3月31日木曜　天気　曇

午前中と夜シェイクスピアを読んだ。チャペルから小包が来たが、コートがきゅうくつすぎたので午後またチャペルに持って行った。『デイビー』[注：デイビッド・カッパーフィールドのこと] を読んだ。

シティから帰って来る途中道を間違えてしまい、警官に何度かストランドへの道を尋ね、ようやくオールド・ストリートの近くでバスに乗ってトッテナムコートロードに行き、それからユーストンまで歩いて、またアデレードまでバスに乗り家に着いた。ユーストンでのバスの中で鈴木氏に偶然会った。

4月

4月1日金曜　天気　晴

午前中と夜シェイクスピアを読んだ。ホイットニー博士を訪ねてカムデンロードに行き、義理の父上ブレイスウォート氏に紹介され、彼は新約聖書のギリシャ語のM.N.Sを見せてくれて、ヘブライ語で「イザヤ書第3章」を読んでくれた。そこでお茶をいただいた。店は閉まっている（グッ

Hampstead Heath.

発信　Letters to home & Dr. Ibuka.
　　　Postals to home, Tachibana Shanghai, Kashiwaguma, Hong Kong.
受信　A letter (April Fool).

4月2日土曜　天気　Fair

Read *Davy* in the morning. Took bath at 11.

In the afternoon went to Charing Cross, bought an English translation of *History of Telemachus* (2d).

4月3日日曜　神武天皇祭　天気　Fair

Easter Sunday

In the morning read Shakespeare & finished *Romeo & Juliet*. In the afternoon took a walk to Primrose Hill, Regent Park & Oxford str., took coffee at Vienna Café. Played chess in the evening.

受信　The Student.

4月4日月曜　天気　Fair rain in the evening

Easter Monday -- Bank Holiday

In the morning read *Othello* & *Davy*.

Received the picture from Mr. Suzuki, sent by Mr. Hirata, Oxford. In the afternoon went to Hampstead Heath to see the crowd mostly of common people & costards. Cocoanut "shies□□□" "Swings," "Marry go rounds," Wheels are the principal pleasure of Easter Monday &tickling with a peacock tail is the characteristic joke of the day. They were munching, drinking, singing & dancing in an utmost joy. They were mostly dressed in light blue & round rimed hat set off with a very large white or black ostrich feathers.

ドフライデーのため)。多くの人々がハムステッド・ヒースに向かっていくのを見た。

4月2日土曜　天気　晴

　午前中『デイビー』を読んだ。11時に入浴。午後はチャリング・クロスに行って『テーレマコスの歴史』の英語版を購入した（2ペンス）。

4月3日日曜　神武天皇祭　天気　晴
イースター・サンデー

　午前中シェイクスピアを読み、『ロミオとジュリエット』を読み終わった。午後はプリムローズ・ヒル、リージェントパーク、オックスフォードストリートまで散歩し、ヴィエナ・カフェでコーヒーを飲んだ。夜はチェスをした。

4月4日月曜　天気　晴夕方雨

　イースターマンデー、バンクホリデー［注：労働者の休日を確保する目的で、銀行を休業にし商業全般が停止する日。年に Easter Monday, Whit-Monday, first Monday in August, Boxing Day の4回ある］
　午前中『オセロ』と『デイビー』を読んだ。
　オックスフォードの平田氏から送られた写真を鈴木氏から受け取った。午後はハムステッド・ヒースに行って、主には庶民や田舎の人たちの人ごみを見た。ココナッツシャイ［注：スタンドに立てたココナッツの実にボールを当てて落とすゲーム］、回転ブランコ、メリーゴーラウンド、観覧車がイースターマンデーの大きな楽しみで、孔雀の羽根でくすぐるのがこの日の特徴的なふざけ方である。人々は大喜びで食べ、飲み、歌い、踊

4月5日火曜　天気　Fair

Read *Davy* –wrote letters & postals – played chess in the evening. Had sore throat, kept indoors all the day.

受信　2 pictorial war reports from Seki, Hiroshima.

4月6日水曜　天気　Very fine

Read *Davy* in the morning. In the afternoon went to see Mr. Oakes & then went with him to see Mr. Maxwell in Cator Avenue, but he was out and met Mrs. Maxwell & son. Bought a Copy of *Graphic*, *Sphere*, & *Black & White* to send to Japan.

Played chess in the evening with Dr. Ritter. Mrs. Moss & Florie started for a Channel island (Sark) where they mean to stay ten days or a fortnight.

4月7日木曜　天気　Fair Hail in the afternoon

Wrote letters in the morning & afternoon. Read *Davy* in the evening. Took a short walk. Mr. Suzuki called. Learned *Anglosaxon* by Dr. Ritter. Played chess.

る。人々はたいてい薄い青の服に、丸い縁取りのある帽子にとても大きな白か黒の駝鳥の羽根を付けている。

バンクホリデーを楽しむ人々(『倫敦名所図絵』より)

4月5日火曜　天気　晴

『デイビー』を読み、書状と葉書を認め、夜はチェスをした。のどが痛くなり、終日家にいた。

4月6日水曜　天気　快晴

午前中は『デイビー』を読んだ。午後はオークス氏に会いに行き、それから彼と一緒にケイターアヴェニューのマックスウェル氏に会いに行ったが、不在でマックスウェル夫人と子息に会った。日本に送るために「グラフィック」「スフィア」「ブラックアンドホワイト」[注：写真雑誌]を1冊ずつ購入した。

夜ドクトル・リットルとチェスをした。モス夫人とフローリーはチャンネル諸島(サーク島)へ出発した。10日から2週間滞在する予定だ。

4月7日木曜　天気　晴午後あられ

午前も午後も書状を認めた。夜は『デイビー』を読んだ。少し散歩した。鈴木氏が来訪。『アングロサクソン』についてドクトル・リットルに教示を受けた。チェスをした。

発信　A postal to Mr. Burnside.
受信　A postal from Mr. Lloyd.

4月8日金曜　天気　Fair

Read *Davy*. Studied *Anglosaxon*. Went to see Dr. Mishima at Gower str. Bought Glossary to Shakespeare's works by Rev. Alexander Dyce. (3s)

発信　Letters to home, Shirani, H.N.C. English Speaking Society.
　　　Postals to home & Seki.
　　　Pictures to home, Hojo, & Seki.
受信　A letter from Yokohama Specie Bank (London) including Check (£ 89-15-4)
　　　A postal from Mr. Hara.

4月9日土曜　天気　Fair

Read *Dav*y & studied *Anglo-saxon* in the morning. Went to Exeter Hall to the monthly meeting & took lesson from Mr. Burnside there before meeting. Met Mr. Nakano(?) sent by the Dept. of Education for the study of English. Took dinner at the Japanese Club at 39, King's street.

受信　A letter from home.

4月10日日曜　天気　Fair　寒暖　Warm

Studied *Anglo-saxon* in the morning & went to Church. In the afternoon attended the lecture on Crammer & the Reformation in England by Mr. Maxwell held in a backroom of Lyndhurst church. Accompanying Mr. Maxwell to his house took tea there & saw two young gentlemen with who went to Xian Policemen's meeting near Maitland Park Rd. The congregation was mostly of common people & a

4月8日金曜　天気　晴

『デイビー』を読んだ。『アングロサクソン』を勉強した。ガワーストリートにミシマ博士に会いに行った。アレクサンダー・ダイス牧師によるシェイクスピア作品の用語集を購入した（3シリング）。

4月9日土曜　天気　晴

午前中は『デイビー』を読み、『アングロサクソン』を勉強した。エクセターホールに月例会に行って、そこで月例会の前にバーンサイド氏からレッスンを受けた。文部省から英語研究のために派遣されたナカノ（？）氏に会った。キングスストリート39番の日本クラブで夕食を取った。

4月10日日曜　天気　晴　寒暖　暖

午前中『アングロサクソン』を勉強し、教会に行った。午後はマックスウェル氏により、リンドハースト教会の奥の部屋で行われたるクラマーとイングランドの改革に関する講義に出席した。マックスウェル氏と共に彼の家を訪ね、そこでお茶をいただき、2人の若い紳士に会った。彼らと一緒にメイトランドパークロードの近くのキリスト教徒の警官の集会に行った。会衆は主に庶民であり、大変興味深い集会だった。

very interesting meeting.

　　4月11日月曜　天気　Very fine　寒暖　Warm

　　Read *Davy* in the morning. In the afternoon went to Kent to see the Popes. The weather was very fine. Gardens were full of beautiful flowers, some trees were in blossoms, apple trees were jut beginning to bud, tall pine trees & the singing of sky-larks reminded the admirer his far off native country. Ploughmen were simple & nice to greet the stranger in their most simple way, men are most natural where nature is not polluted by human acts.

発信　A letter to Miss A. Waber.
受信　A letter from Miss Waber.

　　4月12日火曜　天気　Fair　寒暖　Warm

　　Read *Davy* in the morning. Went to Miss Waber to take lesson.

発信　Postals to Mr. Lloyd & Mr. Ibaraki.
受信　A letter from Miss Waber.
　　　A postal from Mr. S. Kato.

　　4月13日水曜　天気　Fair　寒暖　Warm

　　Read *Davy* in the morning & read *Anglo-saxon* & wrote composition in the afternoon. Wrote letters & read *Davy* in the evening. Reported
　Russian warship, the Petropavlovsk, blown up, Admiral Makaroff drowned, officers & sailors (700) lost, cause unknown.

受信　A letter from Mr. Ibaraki.

4月11日月曜　天気　快晴　寒暖　暖

　午前中は『デイビー』を読んだ。午後はケントに行きポープ家を訪ねた。天気はよかった。庭園には美しい花があふれ、花が咲いている木もあり、りんごの木はつぼみが膨らみ始めたところであった。高い松の木とヒバリのさえずりに感嘆し、遠く離れた祖国を思い出した。農民は素朴で愛想よく、何のてらいもなく挨拶してくれる。自然が人間の行いに汚されていないところでは、人間もきわめて自然なのである。

　4月12日火曜　天気　晴　寒暖　暖

　午前中は『デイビー』を読んだ。レッスンを受けにウェイバー嬢のところに行った。

　4月13日水曜　天気　晴　寒暖　暖

　午前中は『デイビー』を読み、午後は『アングロサクソン』を読み、英作文をした。夜は書状を認め、『デイビー』を読んだ。
　ロシアの戦艦「ペトロパブロフスク」が爆発、マカロフ司令官は溺死、士官と水夫700名が行方不明、原因不明。

4月14日木曜　天気　Fair　寒暖　Warm

Read *Davy* in the morning. Went to Miss Waber's to take lesson in the afternoon.

発信　A letter & postal to home.
　　　Newspaper to Mr. Hojo.

4月15日金曜　天気　Rain　寒暖　Warm

In the morning read *Pericle Prince of Tyne*, a novel by George Wilkins (Printed in 1608 – Reprinted 1857). Went to see Mr. Ibaraki. Read *Pericles* whole afternoon, & read through in the evening.

受信　A postal from Dr. Whitney.

4月16日土曜　天気　Fair

In the morning read *Davy* & made preparation for the lesson afternoon. Mr. Burnside came & gave a lesson in the afternoon. Read in the evening.

受信　A postal from Miss Pope.
　　　A postal from Florie.

4月17日日曜　天気　Fair

Read *Davy* in the morning. In the afternoon attended Mr. Maxwell's class; Went to tea to Mr. Mailis & then went to the Congregational Chappell at Maitland Park Rd.

4月18日月曜　天気　Fair

In the morning read *Davy*. The destruction of Petropavlovsk was confirmed to be caused by a mine laid by Japanese in today's paper.

4月14日木曜　天気　晴　寒暖　暖
　午前中『デイビー』を読んだ。午後はレッスンを受けにウェイバー嬢のところへ行った。

4月15日金曜　天気　雨　寒暖　暖
　午前中ジョージ・ウィルキンスの小説『ペリクリーズ・タインの王子』（1608年印刷、1857年再印刷）を読んだ。茨木氏に会いに行った。午後もずっと『ペリクリーズ』を読み、夜に読了した。

4月16日土曜　天気　晴
　午前中『デイビー』を読み、午後のレッスンの準備をした。午後はバーンサイド氏がレッスンをしにやって来た。夜は読書をした。

4月17日日曜　天気　晴
　午前中は『デイビー』を読んだ。午後マックスウェル氏の授業に参加した。メイリス氏のところにお茶を行き、それからメイトランドパークロードの会衆派教会に行った。

4月18日月曜　天気　晴
　午前中は『デイビー』を読んだ。今朝の新聞で、戦艦「ペトロパブロフスク」は日本が埋設した水雷で爆沈したことが確認された。翌日の授業の

Made preparation for the next day's lesson.

発信　A letter to Dr. Whitney.
　　　A letter to Mrs. Bartrum.
受信　A letter from Mrs. Bartrum.

4月19日火曜　天気　Fair

In the morning went to Waterloo Station to see off Dr. Whitney & family, Dr. Yamazaki & Mr. Ibaraki; Met Mr. Matsui in the station. He has come from the Continent a few days ago.

Bought Marion Crawford's *"Zoroaster"* (1/6). Went to take lesson in the afternoon.

受信　A letter from Mr. Ibaraki.
　　　Composition from the House S &C.

4月20日水曜　天気　Fair　寒暖　Warm

In the morning read *Othello* & *Davy*. In the afternoon went to the Yokohama Specie Bank & received £30 in cash & deposited £59-14-4. Bought a blank calendar. In the evening read *Othello*. Mrs. Moss & Florie returned from Sark a Channel Island.

発信　A postal to Miss Pope.

4月21日木曜　天気　Fair　寒暖　Cold

In the morning read *Othello* & *Davy* In the afternoon read *Davy*. Went to see Mr. Shattack, but he was not at home.

発信　A letter to Mr. Shattack.
受信　A letter from Mrs. Croft (The Landlady of Mr. Ibaraki).

予習をした。

4月19日火曜　天気　晴

　午前中ウォータールー駅にホイットニー博士とご一家、山崎博士と茨木氏を見送りに行った。駅でマツイ氏に会った。彼は2、3日前に大陸からやって来ていた。
　マリオン・クロフォードの『ゾロアスター』を購入した（1シリング6ペンス）。午後はレッスンを受けに行った。

4月20日水曜　天気　晴　寒暖　暖

　午前中は『オセロ』と『デイビー』を読んだ。午後は横浜正金銀行に行って30ポンドを現金で受け取り59ポンド14シリング4ペンスを貯金した。余白だけがあるカレンダーを購入した。夜は『オセロ』を読んだ。モス夫人とフローリーがチャンネル諸島のサーク島から帰って来た。

4月21日木曜　天気　晴　寒暖　寒

　午前中『オセロ』と『デイビー』を読んだ。午後は『デイビー』を読んだ。シャタック氏を訪問したが、不在であった。

4月22日金曜　天気　Rain　寒暖　Cold

Read *Davy* in the morning. Wrote letters in the afternoon. Read *Othello* in the evening.

受信　A postal from Mr. Shattack.

4月23日土曜　天気　Fair

Read *Davy* in the morning. Went to have hair cut. Took bath. Mr. Burnside came in the afternoon to give lesson. Paid him ￡ 1-1-0 for six lessons. Mr. Waber came to board.

4月24日日曜　天気　Fair　寒暖　Cold

In the morning read *Othello* & *Davy*. Went to see Mrs. Croft (Mr. Ibaraki's landlady), but she was not at home. In the afternoon went to attend the class of Mr. Maxwell, then to see Mrs. Bartrum & went to the Parish Church with her family.

4月25日日曜　天気　Fair　寒暖　Cold

In the morning read *Davy,* wrote composition. In the afternoon went to Charing Cross.

4月26日月曜　天気　Fair　寒暖　Cold

In the morning copied composition, wrote letters. In the afternoon went to take lesson. Went to Mrs. Croft, Mr. Ibaraki's landlady. Went to the Library. Wrote a report to be sent to the Minister of Education in Tokyo.

4月27日火曜　天気　Fair

In the morning read *Davy* & wrote a composition on Japanese Art. In the afternoon took a walk to a country road beyond Hampstead Heath.

4月22日金曜　天気　雨　寒暖　寒
　午前中『デイビー』を読んだ。午後は書状を認めた。夜は「オセロ」を読んだ。

4月23日土曜　天気　晴
　午前中『デイビー』を読んだ。散髪に行った。入浴した。バーンサイド氏が午後レッスンのために来訪した。6回のレッスン代として1ポンド1シリング10ペンス払った。ウェイバー氏が下宿しに来た。

4月24日日曜　天気　晴　寒暖　寒
　午前中『オセロ』と『デイビー』を読んだ。クロフト夫人（茨木氏の下宿先の大家夫人）に会いに行ったが、不在だった。午後マックスウェル氏の授業に出席し、それからバートラム夫人を訪問し、ご家族と共に教区教会に行った。

4月25日日曜　天気　晴　寒暖　寒
　午前中『デイビー』を読み、英作文をした。午後はチャリング・クロスへ行った。

4月26日月曜　天気　晴　寒暖　寒
　午前中英作文を書き写し、書状を認めた。午後レッスンを受けに行った。茨木氏の下宿先の大家夫人クロフト夫人を訪ねた。図書館に行った。東京の文部省に送る報告書を書いた。

4月27日火曜　天気　晴
　午前中は『デイビー』を読み、日本の芸術に関する英作文をした。午後はハムステッド・ヒースの向こうの田舎道まで散歩に行った。夜は『デイ

Read *Davy* in the evening.

発信　Letters to home, Midzuki, Department of Education, Mr. Obata (London).
　　Postals to Yamada & Mrs. Ichiai, Midsuashi, Mrs. Pope.

4月28日水曜　天気　Cloudy　寒暖

Read *Davy* in the morning. In the afternoon went to take lesson.

受信　A letter & postal from home (Postal from Tokyo).
　　A letter from Mr. Obata.

4月29日木曜

In the morning read *Davy*. In the afternoon went to Harriet str. (Williams & Norgate) & to Denny & Co. in the Strand & talked about the order from H. N. C. & learnt that they have sent books already & had their bill paid, & they are glad to send books as soon as they get order. Told them to send catalogue to H. N. C. Read *Davy* in the evening.

発信　A postal to Mr. Mimoto.

4月30日金曜　天気　Cloudy

In the morning read *Davy*, wrote composition on Sunday in London. Took bath. In the afternoon Mr. Burnside came to give lesson. Wrote a letter in the evening.

受信　A postal from Mr. Mimoto.

ビー』を読んだ。

　4月28日水曜　天気　曇
　午前中は『デイビー』を読んだ。午後はレッスンを受けに行った。

　4月29日木曜
　午前中は『デイビー』を読んだ。午後はハリエット・ストリート（ウィリアムズ＆ノーゲイト出版社）へ行き、ストランドのデニー社に行って、広島高師からの注文について話し、もうすでに書物を発送したこと、代金が払われていることがわかった。注文を受けると喜んですぐに発送してくれていた。広島高師にカタログを送ってくれるように依頼した。夜は『デイビー』を読んだ。

　4月30日金曜　天気　曇
　午前中は『デイビー』を読み、「ロンドンの日曜日」について英作文をした。入浴した。午後はバーンサイド氏がレッスンに来訪した。午後書状を認めた。

5月

5月1日日曜　天気　Fair　寒暖　Mild

Wrote letters in the morning. In the afternoon went to visit Florie to see Mr. Mimoto in Brondesbury where we saw Mr. Ishii. Took the train from Chalk Farm to Queen's Park on going & took bus from the corner of Walterton Rd. to North Star in Finchly Rd. on coming home.

Reported Japanese victory in the first land campaign near the Yalu!

5月2日月曜　天気　Rain

The report of Japanese victory was confirmed. In the afternoon went to see the Middlesex Hospital in Cleaveland Str. with Dr. Mishima. Dr. Ritter left this morning.

受信　2 Pictorial war reports from Seki, Hiroshima.

5月3日火曜　天気　Fair　寒暖　Mild

In the morning wrote an English composition on "Marseilles." In the afternoon went to take lesson. Went to Camden Theater to see "Geisha." Flo went together.

5月4日水曜　天気　Fair　寒暖　Mild

In the morning wrote letters. In the afternoon went to Westend & bought Sweet's *Anglosaxon Reader* 3/6. In the evening wrote a letter asking for permission for the Educational Department for journey. Read *Paul Patoff, & Davy*.

発信　A letter to Mr. Hirata (Oxford).

5月

5月1日日曜　天気　晴　寒暖　温暖

午前中は書状を認めた。午後はブロンデスベリーの三本氏を訪ねてフローリーのところを訪問し、そこでイシイ氏に会った。行きはチョークファームからクイーンズパークまで列車に乗り、帰りはウォルタートンの角からフィンチリーロードのノーススターまでバスに乗った。

鴨緑江付近での初の地上戦で日本の勝利が報じられた。

5月2日月曜　天気　雨

日本の勝利の報が確認された。午後はミシマ博士とクリーブランドのミドルエセックス病院を見学に行った。ドクトル・リットルは今朝発った。

5月3日火曜　天気　晴　寒暖　温暖

午前中は「マルセイユ」について英作文をした。午後はレッスンを受けに行った。カムデン劇場に「芸者」を観に行った。フローも一緒に行った。

5月4日水曜　天気　晴　寒暖　温暖

午前中書状を認めた。午後はウェストエンドに行って、スウィートの『アングロサクソン・リーダー』を3シリング6ペンスで購入した。夜は文部省に旅の許可を求める書状を認めた。『ポール・パトフ』と『デイビー』を読んだ。

5月5日木曜　天気　Fair　寒暖　Mild

In the morning wrote an English composition on "the Japanese Room." Went to take lesson in the afternoon. Read *Davy* in the evening.

発信　A letter & postal to home.
　　　A letter to Mr. Hojo.
　　　A postal to Seki.
　　　A letter to Monbu sho.
受信　A letter from Ume (from Tokyo dated 4/5).
　　　A letter from Mr. Umeki (Niigata).
　　　A postal from Monbu sho.
　　　The student, & Shirogane gakuho.

5月6日金曜　天気　Fair

Read *Davy* in the morning. Made some preparation for the next day's lesson. Japanese victory in the Yalu reported.

受信　A letter from Mr. Hirata (Oxford).

5月7日土曜　天気　Fair　寒暖　午後2時50°＋

Read *Davy* in the morning. Took bath. Mr. Burnside came to give lesson in the afternoon. The blockading of Port Arthur reported.

受信　A letter from Mr. Hirata (Oxford).
　　　A letter from Hatsuzo (?).
　　　A postal from Mr. Fukata.

5月8日日曜　天気　Rain little　寒暖　Cold 2p.m. 45°

Read *Davy* in the morning. In the afternoon went to see Mr. Matsui in Eccleston Square, then to the Vienna Coffee to see Dr. Ritter to hand the

5月5日木曜　天気　晴　寒暖　温暖
　午前中は「日本の部屋」について英作文を書いた。午後はレッスンを受けに行った。夜は『デイビー』を読んだ。

5月6日金曜　天気　晴
　午前中は『デイビー』を読んだ。翌日のレッスンの予習をした。鴨緑江における日本の勝利が報じられた。

5月7日土曜　天気　晴　寒暖　午後2時50°強
　午前中は『デイビー』を読んだ。入浴した。午後バーンサイド氏がレッスンをしに訪れた。旅順の封鎖が報じられた。

5月8日日曜　天気　小雨　寒暖　寒　午後2時45°
　午前中は『デイビー』を読んだ。午後はエクラストンスクエアにミツイ氏に会いに行き、それからドクトル・リットルに会いにヴィエナ・カフェ

MS from Mr. Hirata, lent him £ 2.

5月9日月曜　天気　Cloudy　寒暖　2 p.m. 54°　Cold

Read *Davy* in the morning. Evacuation of Newchang by Russians; isolation of Port Arthur; investment of Daling reported.

Coldest May days since seventeen years, it is said. Yesterday was the coldest in past few days.

受信　2 postal from Ume (Tokyo 7/4).
　　　A letter from Shirani (Utsunomiya).
　　　A money order(£ 1-18-9) from Nippon Ginko.

5月10日火曜　天気　Rain a.m. Fair p.m.　寒暖　Mild 54°　2 p.m.

In the morning read the *Paul Patoff*, wrote composition on the Educational system of Japan. In the afternoon went to take lesson.

Sir Henry M. Stanley, the great explorer, died this morning in his residence in London, aged 63(?).

Read in the evening. Paid £ 1-5-0 to Miss A.Weber for 10 lessons.

5月11日水曜　天気　Cloudy　寒暖　Mild

Read *Davy* in the morning. Wrote composition on "The Sport in Japan." Read *Davy* in the evening.

5月12日木曜　天気　Cloudy　寒暖　Mild

In the morning read *Paul Putoff*. Copied the composition. In the afternoon went to take lesson. Read *Davy* in the evening.

受信　A letter from Denny & CO.

に行き、平田氏からのMSを手渡し、2ポンド貸した。

5月9日月曜　天気　曇　寒暖　午後2時54°　寒
午前中は『デイビー』を読んだ。ロシア軍はNewchangから退避し、旅順は孤立し、大陵は包囲されていると報じられた。
この17年で5月としては一番寒い日とのことである。昨日はこの数日で最も寒かった。

5月10日火曜　天気　午前雨　午後晴．寒暖　温暖　午後2時54°
午前中は、『ポール・パトフ』を読んで、日本の教育制度について英作文をした。午後はレッスンを受けに行った。
偉大な探検家のサー・ヘンリー・M・スタンレーが今日ロンドンの自宅で亡くなった。享年63（？）。
夜は『デイビー』を読んだ。A・ウェイバー嬢に10回のレッスン料として1ポンド5シリング払った。

5月11日水曜　天気　曇　寒暖　温暖
午前中は『デイビー』を読んだ。「日本のスポーツ」について英作文をした。夜は『デイビー』を読んだ。

5月12日木曜　天気　曇　寒暖　温暖
午前中は『ポール・パトフ』を読んだ。英作文を清書した。午後はレッスンを受けに行った。夜は『デイビー』を読んだ。

5月13日金曜　天気　Cloudy　寒暖　Mild

Read *Davy* in the morning. A Japanese destroyer reported blown up. Read *Davy* in the evening.

It was confirmed that a Japanese torpedo-boat was blown up in Kerr bay while trying to remove a mechanical mine laid by Russians.

発信　A postal to Denny & CO.

5月14日土曜　天気　Fair　寒暖　Mild

In the morning read *Davy*. Took bath. In the afternoon went to Exeter Hall, the Strand, Violet went to Crystal Palace with her mother & other children to receive the Certificate.

受信　A postal from Denny & CO.

5月15日日曜　天気　Fair　寒暖　Mild

Went to Lamdhurst Chapel in the morning. Took dinner at Mr. Suzuki's lodging.

With Mr. Suzuki & two English gentlemen lodging in the same house went to Hampton Court, saw noted Chestnut tree in full bloom in Rugby Park. Saw Hampton Court Palace, splendid old tapestries in the banqueting Hall, beautiful paintings in kings' and Queen's private rooms & bedrooms.

It has a beautiful garden. There were many Japanese gold fish in the pond. This is the largest Royal Palace [Hoi p.3] in England & was originally founded in 1515 by Cardinal Walsey, the favorite of Henry Ⅷ, and was afterward presented by him to the king.

It was subsequently occupied by Cromwell, the Stuarts, William III., & the first two monarchs of the house of Hanover. Since the time of George II, Hampton Court has earned to be royal residence, and over 800

5月13日金曜　天気　曇　寒暖　温暖

午前中は『デイビー』を読んだ。日本の駆逐艦が爆破されたと報じられた。夜『デイビー』を読んだ。

日本の日本の水雷艇がロシアが埋設した機械水雷を除去する作業中にKerr湾で爆破されたことが確認された。

5月14日土曜　天気　晴　寒暖　温暖

午前中は『デイビー』を読んだ。入浴した。午後はストランドのエクセターホールに行った。ヴァイオレットは母親と一緒に水晶宮［注：1851年にロンドンのハイド・パークで開催された第1回万国博覧会の会場として建てられた建築物］に行き、他の子供たちは成績表をもらいに行った。

5月15日日曜　天気　晴　寒暖　温暖

午前中ラムドハースト・チャペルに行った。鈴木氏の下宿でディナーを取った。

鈴木氏と同じ家に下宿している2人のイギリス人紳士と一緒にハンプトンコートに行き、ラグビーパークで有名な栗の木の花が満開になっているのを見た。ハンプコートパレス、バンケットホールの素晴らしい古いタペストリー、王と女王の私室と寝室の美しい絵画を見学した。

美しい庭園があった。池には日本の金魚がたくさんいた。ここは英国で最も大きい王宮で、［補遺、p.3］　もともと1515年にヘンリー8世のお気に入りだったウルジー枢機卿によって作られたが、後に彼によって王に贈呈された。

後にクロムウェル、スチュアート家、ウィリアム3世、ハノーバー王朝の最初の2人の王によって占領された。ジョージ2世の時代から、ハンプトンコートは王宮で、1000室の中の800室以上が今は王家の貴族の別荘として一括して使われている。そこに行くのにハムステッド・ヒースから

of its 1000 rooms are now occupied in suites by aristocratic pensions of the Crown. To go there took train from Hampstead Heath Station to Richmond, then electric tram. This is situated near the banks of the Thames about 15 miles up from London. The scenery about here is beautiful.

5月16日月曜　天気　Fair　寒暖　Warm

Read *Davy* in the morning, went to Mrs. Maxwell's to tea & stayed till after dinner.

発信　A letter to Mrs. Maxwell.

5月17日火曜　天気　Fair　寒暖　Warm

In the morning read *Davy* & wrote composition about the flowers of Japan. Went to take lesson.

Took walk to the Hampstead Heath in the evening.

ハムステッド・ヒース（『倫敦名所図絵』より）

5月18日水曜　天気　Fair

In the morning read *Davy*, wrote letters.

リッチモンドまで列車に乗り、それから電気式の列車に乗った。ここはテムズ川岸にあり、ロンドンから15マイル上流である。このあたりの景色は美しい。

5月16日月曜　天気　晴　寒暖　暖
　午前中は『デイビー』を読んだ。マックスウェル夫人をお茶に訪ね、夕食後まで滞在した。

5月17日火曜　天気　晴　寒暖　暖
　午前中は『デイビー』を読み、日本の花に関して英作文をした。レッスンを受けに行った。
　夜ハムステッド・ヒースに散歩に行った。

現在のハムステッド・ヒース

5月18日水曜　天気　晴
　午前中『デイビー』を読み、書状を認めた。

発信　A postal to Dr. Ritter.
　　　A postal to Mr. Hirata (Oxford).

5月19日木曜　天気　Fair　寒暖　Warm

In the morning wrote a composition on Bushy Park & Hampton Court Palace. Went to the Maxwells & played cricket. In the evening went to "Vienna Café" to see Dr. Ritter & Collier's Notes on Shakespeare, given by him.

Sent telegram to Mr. Hirata, Oxford.

Japanese warships the Hatsuse & a cruiser the Yoshino, reported blown up off Port Arthur by contact mines laid by the Russians – nearly 700 lives lost.

発信　A postal to Monbusho.
　　　A postal to Mr. Hirata (Oxford).
　　　Receipt to Chyuo Kinko.
　　　A letter & picture book to home.
　　　A letter to Messrs. Elliot & Smith.
　　　A picture book to Hatsuzo.
　　　The Daily Telegraph to Mr. Hojo.
　　　A postal to home.
　　　A. telegram to Mr. Hirata. 10 p.m.
受信　A letter from Ume (Tokyo 15/4).
　　　A postal from Mr. Yazima (Usawa).
　　　A letter from Mr. Mimoto.(Mail list).
　　　A postal from Dr. Ritter.
　　　A telegram from Mr. Hirata, Oxford. 8 p.m.

5月20日金曜　天気　Fair　寒暖　Warm

Taking 9.50 train at Paddington Station, went to Stratford-on-Avon

5月19日木曜　天気　晴　寒暖　暖

　午前中ブッシー・パークとハンプトン・コートについて英作文をした。マックスウェル家を訪ね、クリケットをした。夜はドクトル・リットルに会いにヴィエナ・カフェに行ってコリアーによるシェイクスピアの注釈をもらった。

　オックスフォードの平田氏に電報を打った。

　日本の戦艦「初瀬」と巡洋艦「吉野」が旅順沖でロシア軍に埋設された触雷に爆破され、700名近くが死亡したと報じられている。

左・ホーリートリニティ教会（Sidney Lee 著 *Stratford-on-Avon* Cambridge University Press, 1890 内の Edward Hull によるイラスト）右・シェイクスピアの墓（現在）

5月20日金曜　天気　晴　寒暖　暖

　パディントン駅で9時50分の列車に乗り、ストラットフォード・オン・

(100+ ms). Saw Shakespeare's birth place museums, Parish Church where the poet is buried, the epitaph on the tomb:

> Good frend, for Jesus sak forbeare
> To dig the dust enclosed heare:
> Bleste be ye man yt spares thes stones,
> And curst be he yt moves my bones.

Stayed at Mr. Cook's (apartment), Old Town.

発信　Postals to home & Mr. Hojo.

「アン・ハサウェイの家」の内部（Sidney Lee 著 *Stratford-on-Avon* より Edward Hull のイラスト）

5月21日土曜　天気　Rain　寒暖　Cold

　Stratford-on-Avon. In the morning went to Shakespeare's Birthplace again & saw the librarian Mr. Richard Savage who showed us several manuscripts & took us (Dr. Jacob Ritter, an Austrian, Mr. Kiichi Hirata &

エイボン（100マイル以上の距離）に行った。シェイクスピアの生家のミュージアム、シェイクスピアが埋葬されている教区教会、墓碑銘を見た。

　良き友よ、イエスのために控えよ、
　ここに葬られた亡骸を掘ることを。
　この墓石守るものに祝福あれ。
　わが骨動かすものに呪いあれ。

　オールドタウンのクック氏宅（アパート）に宿泊した。

シェイクスピアの生家（Sidney Lee 著 *Stratford-on-Avon* より Edward Hull のイラスト）

5月21日土曜　天気　雨　寒暖　寒
　ストラットフォード・オン・エイボン。午前中は再度シェイクスピアの生家を訪れ、ライブラリアンのリチャード・サビッジ氏に会い、彼がいくつもの原稿を見せてくれて、私たち（オーストリア人のドクトル・ヤコ

myself) to Anne Hathaway's Cottage, where the great poet used to court for his future wife. Saw many old things. On leaving Miss Anne Hathaway Baker (she is named after old Anne Hathaway) the daughter of the man who looks after the Cottage picked twigs of the rosemary growing close to the cottage & gave it to each of us as a memory of our visit.

In the afternoon, [continue to ap p.4]went to Shakespeare Memorial, saw pictures, books &c. The librarian showed us a copy of the first folio, which is said to be existing not more than 15 copies in the world, & also several copies of first quartos which are all invaluable & very rare.

発信　Postal to home, Mr. Tanaka (Kanagawa).
　　　Mr. Kurihara (Hiroshima)

「アン・ハサウェイの家」（Sidney Lee 著 *Stratford-on-Avon* より Edward Hull のイラスト）

ブ・リットルと平田喜一氏と私）をアン・ハサウェイの家に連れて行ってくれた。そこが偉大な詩人シェイクスピアが将来の妻に何度も求婚した場所である。多くの古いものを見た。去り際に、この家の世話をしている人の娘であるアン・ハサウェイ・ベーカー嬢（元祖アン・ハサウェイにちなんで名づけられた）が、家の近くに生えているローズマリーを摘んで、訪問の記念に私たちの1人ひとりに渡してくれた。

　午後は［補遺4頁に続く］シェイクスピア・メモリアルに行って、写真や本などを見た。ライブラリアンはファースト・フォリオを1枚見せてくれた、それは世界に多くて15枚しか現存していないと言われている。また、ファースト・クアルトを数枚見せてくれたが、それらはすべて非常に貴重で希少なものである。

現在の「アン・ハサウェイの家」

5月22日日曜　天気　Cloudy　寒暖　less cold 56° 2 p.m
Whit Sunday

Stratford-on-Avon. In the morning took walk to Shottery to see the Cottage once more from the outside. Took 10.50 train at Stratford Station. Got at Oxford 1 p.m., took lunch at Mr. Hirata's. Took walk to the Addison Walk went to see Max Muller's grave, took walk to the park. Left Oxford 5.50 p.m., got at Paddington Station at 9 p.m. got home 10 1/2.

5月23日月曜　天気　Fair　寒暖　Warmer 70° 2 p.m.
Whit Monday

This is another Bank holiday. Hampstead Heath is again crowded by common people. In the morning took bath. Read *Davy*. Went to the Heath after tea. The aspect of the Heath is same as in the time of Easter Monday.

5月24日火曜　天気　Rain

In the morning read *Paul Patoff* & wrote a composition on "Ambition." In the afternoon went to take lesson.

発信　A postal to Herr Toda.
　　　A postal to Mr. Kodama.
受信　A postal from Herr Toda.

5月25日水曜　天気　Fair　寒暖　Warm

In the morning read *Davy*, wrote letters.

5月26日木曜　天気　Rain　寒暖　Warmer 73°

In the morning wrote a composition on Stratford-on-Avon. In the

5月22日日曜　天気　曇　寒暖　寒さやわらぐ　午後2時56°
聖霊降臨祭
　ストラットフォード・オン・エイボン。午前中「アン・ハサウェイの家」を外からもう一度見るためにショッタリーまで歩いて行った。ストラットフォード駅から10時50分の列車に乗った。オックスフォードに午後1時に付き、平田氏宅で昼食を取った。アディソン・ウォークを散歩し、マックス・ミューラーの墓へ行き、公園まで歩いて行った。オックスフォードを午後5時50分に出発し、パディントン駅に午後9時に着いた。10時半帰宅。

5月23日月曜　天気　晴　寒暖　気温上り午後2時70°
聖霊降臨祭翌日
　今日はまたバンク・ホリデーである。ハムステッド・ヒースはまた庶民でいっぱいだった。午前中入浴した。『デイビー』を読んだ。お茶の後でハムステッド・ヒースに行った。ハムステッド・ヒースの状況はイースターマンデーの時と同じである。

5月24日火曜　天気　雨
　午前中『ポール・パトフ』を読み、「大志」について英作文をした。午後はレッスンを受けに行った。

5月25日水曜　天気　晴　寒暖　暖
　午前中は『デイビー』を読み、書状を認めた。

5月26日木曜　天気　雨　寒暖　いっそう暖　73°
　午前中はストラットフォード・オン・エイボンについて英作文をした。

afternoon went to take lesson.

発信　A letter & postal to home.
　　　A postal to Mr. Hirata.
受信　Anglosaxon Gospel (Yulu) from Mr. Hirata.
　　　Pictoral War news from Mr. Hojo.
　　　Letters from Messrs. Nagaya, Shirani, Obana, & Imanishi.
　　　Postals from Yoshi & Nobu.

　5月27日金曜　天気　A little rain　寒暖　Warm

In the morning went to see the Church of England Girls' High School. Upper Baker Street, Miss Strong is the head teacher. Wrote postals in the afternoon. Went to a Literary Entertainment at Mr. Maxwell's in the evening.

　Capture of Rim Chan reported (officially).

発信　Postals to home (4).
　　　Postal to Messrs. Hojo, Shirani Nagaya (1).
　　　Picture & a postal to Mr. Obana.
　　　A letter to Mrs. Taylor.
受信　Picture from Ume.
　　　War picture from Mr. Obana.
　　　A letter from Mrs. Taylor.

　5月28日土曜　皇后陛下御誕辰　天気　Cloudy　寒暖　62°

In the morning made some preparation for the lesson afternoon.
　Mr. Burnside came to give lesson in the afternoon. Read *Davy* in the evening.

午後はレッスンを受けに行った。

5月27日金曜　天気　小雨　寒暖　暖
　午前中チャーチ・オブ・イングランド女子高校を見学に行った。アッパー・ベイカー・ストリートにあり、ストロング嬢が教頭先生である。午後は葉書を認めた。夜はマックスウェル氏宅に「文学の楽しみの会」に行った。
　Rim Chan の占領が報じられた（公式に）。

5月28日土曜　皇后陛下御誕辰　天気　曇　寒暖　62°
午前中は午後のレッスンの予習をした。
午後バーンサイド氏がレッスンをしに来た。夜は『デイビー』を読んだ。

受信　A postal from Dr. Ritter.

5月29日日曜　天気　Fair　寒暖　67°

In the morning read *Davy*. Took a walk to Hampstead Heath. Went to the Taylors, Heath Hurst Rd. to late tea in the afternoon. Went to the Vienna Café to see Dr. Ritter.

Read the Yomiuri in the evening.

5月30日月曜　天気　Fair　寒暖　70° 2 p.m.

Read *Davy* in the morning. Took bath. Went to the Maxwells, played cricket.

受信　A postal from Mr. Kodama.

5月31日火曜　天気　Foul　寒暖　62° 2 p.m.

In the morning wrote a composition on "Reading." Went to take lesson in the afternoon. Read *Davy* in the evening.

6月

6月1日水曜　天気　Foul

In the morning, went to see Bedford College for Women, saw Classrooms, Laboratories, Library, & students' rooms. Talked with Miss Ethel Hurlbatt, the principal, was much interested. This is a non-denominational College. Number of students 270, 40 of whom are boarders. No religious exercise, except private bible reading & prayer in the morning to which attendance is optional. No special speech on moral culture is given. Morality is based on "honour & responsibility."

Daluy rep'd captured.

5月29日日曜　天気　晴　寒暖　67°
　午前中『デイビー』を読んだ。ハムステッド・ヒースを散歩した。テイラー家に行った。午後ヒースハーストロードに遅いお茶に行った。ドクトル・リットルに会いにヴィエナ・カフェに行った。

　5月30日月曜　天気　晴　寒暖　午後2時70°
　午前中『デイビー』を読んだ。入浴した。マックスウェル家へ行きクリケットをした。

　5月31日火曜　天気　荒天　寒暖　午後2時62°
　午前中「読書」に関して英作文をした。午後はレッスンを受けに行った。夜は『デイビー』を読んだ。

6月

　6月1日水曜　天気　荒天
　午前中、ベッドフォード女子大学を訪ね、教室、研究室、図書館、学生の部屋を見学した。校長エセル・ハルバット嬢と話をした。大変興味深く感じた。ここは無宗派の大学である。学生数は270人でその内40名は寄宿舎にいる。どんな宗教的な学習もないが、ただ個人的に聖書を読んだり、朝の祈りへの参加は自由である。道徳的な文化に関しては特別な話はない。道徳観というのは「名誉と責任感」に基づくものである。
　Daluy が占領されたと報じられた。

発信　A letter to Mrs. M Bartrum.
受信　A letter from Mrs. Bartrum.

６月２日木曜　天気　Cloudy

Wrote a composition in the form of a letter about female education in England. Went to take lesson in the afternoon. Read
Davy, and finished it.

６月３日金曜　天気　Fair　寒暖　Warm

In the morning wrote letters. Read Shakespeare in the afternoon.

発信　A postal to Dr. Ritter.
受信　Postals from Mr. Burnside.
　　　from Messrs. Suzuki & Hirata (Oxford).

６月４日土曜　天気　Fair　寒暖　Warm

In the morning wrote letters. Took bath. In the afternoon read Shakespeare & c.

受信　A postal from Ume (Tokyo).

６月５日日曜　天気　Fair　寒暖　Warm

In the morning read *Zoroaster*. Went to Congregational Chapel but no seat, went to Hampstead Heath. Had made an arrangement of going to Brighton today, but Dr. Ritter failed to write about the time of the train.

Took walk to Primrose Hill, saw a beautiful sunset.

６月６日月曜　天気　Fair　寒暖　Warm

In the morning read *Zoroaster* & c. In the afternoon read *Zoroaster* & c. Wrote composition on Ladies' accomplishment in Japan, in the evening.

6月2日木曜　天気　曇
英国の女子教育について手紙の形式で英作文をした。午後はレッスンを受けに行った。
『デイビー』を読み、読了した。

6月3日金曜　天気　晴　寒暖　暖
午前中書状を認めた。午後はシェイクスピアを読んだ。

6月4日土曜　天気　晴　寒暖　暖
午前中は書状を認めた。入浴した。午後はシェイクスピアその他を読んだ。

6月5日日曜　天気　晴　寒暖　暖
午前中『ゾロアスター』を読んだ。会衆派チャペルに行ったが席がなく、ハムステッド・ヒースに行った。今日ブライトンに行く計画を立てていたが、ドクトル・リットルが列車の時間について書いていなかった。
プリムローズ・ヒルを散歩し、美しい夕陽を見た。

6月6日月曜　天気　晴　寒暖　暖
午前中『ゾロアスター』等を読んだ。午後は『ゾロアスター』等を読んだ。夜は「日本における女性の偉業」について英作文をした。

発信　A letter to Koidzumi.

　　　Postals to Katsunori, Shinowara.

　　　Daily telegraphs to Fumiyasu, Obana.

受信　The Student.

　　　Postal from Kurihara.

　　　A letter from Koidzumi (stud).

　　　A postal from Dr. Ritter.

6月7日火曜　天気　Fair

Wrote letters & postals. Went to take lesson in the afternoon.

発信　A box of note paper to Mr. Suzuki (Oxford).

　　　A postal to Williams & Norgate.

受信　A letter from Mr. Suzuki (Oxford).

　　　Grammar of Old English (Cook) from Williams & Norgate.

6月8日水曜　天気　Fair

Spent the whole morning in reading *Paul Patoff*.

　In the afternoon went to Williams & Norgate to pay the bill (5/) for Cook's *Gram. of Old English*. Went to Denny & CO, saw Mr. Denny, had a child's book sent to Japan, 2/8. Went to Vienna Café to see Dr. Ritter, but he was not there, left a note. Bought Anewdale's English Dictionary 2/-. *Hamlet* 6^D, *Macbeth* 3^D.

発信　A letter to home.

　　　Postals to Kurihara, Koidzumi & Miss Kurimult.

受信　A letter from Dr. Ritter.

　　　A postal from home.

6月7日火曜　天気　晴
手紙と葉書を認めた。午後はレッスンを受けに行った。

6月8日水曜　天気　晴
午前中はずっと『ポール・パトフ』を読んだ。
午後はウィリアムズ・アンド・ノーゲイト出版社にクックの『古英語の文法』の代金（5シリング）を払いに行った。デニー社に行き、デニー氏に会い、児童書を日本に送ってもらった（2シリング8ペンス）。ヴィエナ・カフェにドクトル・リットルに会いに行ったが、彼はそこにはいなかったので、メモを残した。アニューデイルの英語辞書を購入した（2シリング）。『ハムレット』6ペンス、『マクベス』3ペンス。

6月9日木曜　天気　Fair

Wrote a composition in the morning, had a visit from Mr. Nagano, took lunch together.

Went to take lesson in the afternoon. Went to see Mr. Lloyd on the way home. Read *Zoroaster* in the evening.

6月10　金曜　天気　Cloudy

In the morning went to see Church of England Girls' High School, Graham Str. Eton Square. Saw the classes of Elocution, Eng. Lit., Singing, Bible. Met Miss Lewis, the principal.

In the afternoon went to see Miss Snowdon, Putney. Went to the Nihon Jin Kuai & took Japanese Dinner with Mr. Nagano, Captain & Mrs. Lacock.

発信　A postal to Mr. Burnside.
受信　A postal and Yomiuri Shinbun from Mr. Suzuki (Oxford).

6月11日土曜　天気　Cloudy　寒暖　Cold

In the morning read *Zoroaster*, took bath.

In the afternoon went to the monthly meeting of the Japanese Christian Union in Exeter Hall. Bought a Leather belt (2/6).

Read *Zoroaster* in the evening.

Boys and nurses collect money in the street for hospitals for the next day is Hospital Sunday.

受信　A postal & A parcel (Book) from Mr. Kodama (New Castel-on-Tyne)

6月12日日曜　天気　Fair

Hospital Sunday

Went to Lyndhurst Church, but no seat. Took a walk to Oak Park.

6月9日木曜　天気　晴

午前中は英作文をした。永野氏が来訪し、昼食をともにした。

午後はレッスンを受けに行った。帰路ロイド氏に会いに行った。夜は『ゾロアスター』を読んだ。

6月10日金曜　天気　曇

午前中イートンスクエアのグレアムストリートにあるチャーチ・オブ・イングランド女子高校を見学に行った。発声法、英文学、歌唱、聖書の授業を見学した。校長のルイス嬢に会った。

午後はプトニーへスノードン嬢に会いに行った。日本人会へ行き永野氏、ラコック大尉夫妻と日本食の夕食を共にした。

6月11日土曜　天気　曇　寒暖　寒

午前中は『ゾロアスター』を読んで、入浴した。

午後は日本人キリスト教徒ユニオンの月例会にエクセターホールに行った。皮のベルトを購入した（2シリング6ペンス）。

夜は『ゾロアスター』を読んだ。

翌日が「ホスピタル・サンデー」であるため、男子と看護婦たちが通りで病院のための募金をしていた。

6月12日日曜　天気　晴

ホスピタル・サンデー

リンドハースト教会に行ったが、席がなかった。オークパークに散歩に

Mr. Mimoto called in the afternoon. Read *Zoroaster* & Hart's *Grammar*.

6月13日月曜　天気　Fair　寒暖　Cold

In the morning read *Zoroaster* &c. In the afternoon went to the Maxwells stayed to dinner.

発信　A letter to Mr. Hart.
　　　A postal to Mr. Kodama (New Castle on Tyne).
　　　A postal to Mr. Suzuki.

6月14日火曜　天気　Rain

In the morning wrote a composition, in the afternoon went to take lesson. Read *Zoroaster* in the evening.

受信　A postal from Dr. Ritter.

6月15日水曜　天気　Foul

In the morning read Hart's *Grammar*, wrote letters. The afternoon same. Read *Zoroaster* (finished), &c. in the evening. Took boots to the shoemaker to have heels repaired.

6月16日木曜　天気　Fair

In the morning wrote exercises. In the afternoon went to take lesson. Read *Grammar*.

Japanese Transports reported sunk by Vladivostac Fleet in Korean strait. Japanese victory in Wa-fuan-Otien reported.

An excursion steamer with Sunday school children & mothers in New York reported taken fire & nearly a thousand of children & women burnt or drowned. A shocking disaster!

行った。三本氏が午後来訪した。『ゾロアスター』とハート著の『文法書』を読んだ。

6月13日月曜　天気　晴　寒暖　寒
午前中『ゾロアスター』その他を読んだ。午後はマックスウェル家に行き夕食まで滞在した。

6月14日火曜　天気　雨
午前中英作文をした。午後はレッスンを受けに行った。夜は『ゾロアスター』を読んだ。

6月15日水曜　天気　荒天
午前中ハート著の『文法書』を読んで、書状を認めた。午後も同様。夜は『ゾロアスター』（読了した）その他を読んだ。かかとの修理にブーツを靴屋に持って行った。

6月16日木曜　天気　晴
午前中は課題を書いた。午後はレッスンを受けに行った。『文法書』を読んだ。

日本の輸送船がウラジオストック艦隊に朝鮮海峡で沈没させられたと報じられている。日本の Wa-fuan-Otien における勝利が報じられている。

ニューヨークで日曜学校の子供たちと母親の乗った回遊帰船が火災を起こし、1000人近い子供と婦人たちが焼死か溺死かしたと報じられている。恐ろしい大惨事である。

発信　Postals to Dr. Ritter & Mr. Lloyd.
　　　A letter to home.
　　　A letter to Mr. Hojo.
受信　A letter from Dr. Lloyd.
　　　3 Postals from home.
　　　2 letters from home (dated 8/5 & 13/5).
　　　A Postal from Rako.

6月17日金曜　天気　Fair

Wrote letters in the morning. In the afternoon went to see the Exhibition of scholar's work done in London Primary Schools, at the Examination Hall Savoy str. (Victoria Enbankment).

Bought Sheridan's "*School for Scandal*"(2d) & a Picture Book (4d) in Charing Cross.

Went to see Dr. Ritter Charlotte Str. but not at home.

The Hitachimaru, a transport, sunk by Russian Fleet in the Genkai confirmed, & some others reported missing.

受信　"The Student".

6月18日土曜　天気　Fair

Wrote exercises in the morning. Had hair cut. Took bath. Mr. Burnside did not come to give lesson. Boots brought repaired (□□□).

Read *Grammar*s &c.

発信　A letter & a postal to home.
　　　A package of book to home (Photographs together).

6月19日日曜　天気　Fair　寒暖　62°　Cold

In the morning went to Lyndhurst Chapel.

6月17日金曜　天気　晴
　午前中書状を認めた。午後はサボイ・ストリート（ヴィクトリア・エンバンクメント）のエグザミネーション・ホールで開かれたロンドン小学校でなされた学者の仕事の展示会に行った。
　シェリダンの『悪口学校』（2ペンス）と絵本（4ペンス）をチャリングクロスで購入した。
　シャーロット・ストリートのドクトル・リットルに会いに行ったが不在だった。
　輸送船「常陸丸」が玄界灘でロシア艦隊によって沈没させられたことが確認され、他の何隻かが行方不明と報じられた。

 6月18日土曜　天気　晴
　午前中は課題を書いた。散髪した。入浴した。バーンサイド氏がレッスンをしに来なかった。ブーツの修理ができた（□□□）[注：金額か]。
　『文法書』その他を読んだ。

 6月19日日曜　天気　晴　寒暖　62°　寒
　午前中リンドハースト・チャペルに行った。

Wrote an exercise on paraphrasing Wordsworth's Movements to Literary ☐☐. in the afternoon.

Took walk on Hampstead Heath & then went to Bull and Bush with Miss Walker & Messrs. Waldman & Webber.

6月20日月曜　天気　Fair　寒暖　Warm 70°

In the morning copied the exercise. In the afternoon went to take lesson. Read *The Yomiuri* till late in the evening, after talking in this Drawing Room till 11 o'clock.

受信　A parcel of the Jiji & the Yomiuri from Mr. Suzuki (Oxford).
　　　2 postals from home.
　　　A postal from Mr. Tachibana (Shanghai).
　　　A letter from Mr. Burnside.
　　　Afternoon
　　　A letter from Chyuokinko.
　　　Letters from Dr. Ibuka & Mr. Obana.
　　　Postals from Yoshi, Nobu, Seki.
　　　Pictorial Periodical from Mr. Obana.

6月21日火曜　天気　Fair　寒暖　62°

In the morning read *Grammar* & *Paul Patoff* & took walk to Maitland Park Road & further.

Vladivostok Fleet reported returned to the Port!

Took a walk to Primrose Hill & its neighbourhood in the afternoon. Talked till late in the drawing room.

発信　Postals to Mr. Suzuki (Oxford).
　　　Postals to Nagano.

午後はワーズワースの文学□□運動をパラフレーズするという課題を書いた。
　ハムステッド・ヒースへ散歩に行き、それからウォーカー嬢、ウォルドマン氏、ウェーバー氏と共にブル・アンド・ブッシュ［注：パブ＆レストラン］に行った。

6月20日月曜　天気　晴　寒暖　暖　70°
　午前中課題を清書した。午後はレッスンを受けに行った。11時までここの客間で話をした後、夜遅くまで「読売新聞」を読んだ。

6月21日火曜　天気　晴　寒暖　62°
　午前中『文法書』と『ポール・パトフ』を読み、メイトランドパークロードへ、またさらに遠くへ散歩した。
　ウラジオストック艦隊は港へ帰ったとの報道された！
　午後はプリムローズ・ヒルとその近辺を散歩した。客間で遅くまで話をした。

受信　A postal from Dr. Nakagawa.

6月22日水曜　天気　Fair　寒暖　Warm

　　In the morning read *grammar* & c. In the afternoon went to see St. Paul's school, West Kensington & saw the boys (13-19) in the playground playing cricket. Work Rooms, Gymnasium, Swimming Bath & several Class Rooms. Saw Mr. [　　], who has been in Japan for a few months & has a good number of Japanese things in the drawing room. Went to see Dr. Uchida, but not at home.

受信　A telegram from Mr. Nagano

6月23日木曜　天気　Fair　寒暖　Warm

　　Read *Grammar* & wrote compositions in the morning. Went to take lesson in the afternoon. Read *Grammar* &c. in the evening.
　　The Sun rises 3:45, sets 8:19.

受信　Composition from Cosmopolitan Club.
　　　A postal from Mr. Nagano.

6月24日金曜　天気　Fair　寒暖　Warm

　　In the morning read *grammar* & *Paul Patoff*.
　　Made call to Mrs. Bartrum in the afternoon.
　　Port Arthur Fleet sortie & Togo's victory reported.

6月25日土曜　天気　Fair & Shower

　　In the morning read *gramma*r &c. Took bath. Mr. Burnside came to give lesson in the afternoon. Wrote letters in the evening. Bought "Sphere."
　　The Peresvict (?) sunk by Japanese torpedo and another battleship

6月22日水曜　天気　晴　寒暖　暖
　午前中文法書その他を読んだ。午後はウエスト・ケンジントンのセントポールズスクールを見学に行き、13歳から19歳の少年たちが運動場でクリケットをしているのを見た。作業室、体育館、プール、いくつかの教室を見た。［氏名不明］氏に会ったが、彼は2,3か月日本に行ったことがある人物で、応接室に多数の日本の品々を持っていた。
　内田博士に会いに行ったが、不在だった。

6月23日木曜　天気晴　寒暖　暖
　午前中『文法書』を読み、英作文をした。午後はレッスンを受けに行った。夜は『文法書』その他を読んだ。
　太陽は3時45分に昇り、8時19分に沈んだ。

6月24日金曜　天気　晴　寒暖　暖
　午前中『文法書』と『ポール・パトフ』を読んだ。
　午後はバートラム夫人を訪問した。
　旅順の艦隊が出撃し、東郷の勝利が報じられている。

6月25日土曜　天気　晴にわか雨
　午前中『文法書』その他を読んだ。入浴した。午後はバーンサイド氏がレッスンのために来訪した。夜は書状を認めた。「スフィア誌」を購入した。
　ロシアの戦艦ペレスヴィクト号が日本の水雷艇により沈没し、戦艦もう

and a cruiser damaged reported officially.

6月26日日曜　天気　Fair & Shower

In the morning read *Paul Patoff*. Went to the meeting of Ethical Institute in Hampstead conservation. It is non-religious ethical Sunday meeting. They have special hymns & they keep Sunday School for Children.

6月27日月曜　天気　Fair　寒暖　Warm

In the morning read *grammar* & *Paul Patoff*. In the afternoon & evening read *Paul Patoff* & wrote exercise on paraphrasing.

Tolstoi's striking declaration on the enormity of war appeared in today's *Times*.

発信　A postal to Dr. Ritter.
　　　Compositions in envelope to Mr. E Belcher.
受信　A postal from Dr. Ritter.
　　　A letter from Mr. Ingram (Bradfield College, Reading).

6月28日火曜　天気　Fair　寒暖　Warm

In the morning read letters from Japan.

Copied exercise on Paraphrasing. In the afternoon went to take lesson. Read Count Tolstoy's "On War" in *The Times*.

発信　A letter & Sphere to home.
　　　Letters to Nagaya, Hori & Takahashi, Obana.
　　　Postals to Seki, Honma.
受信　A postal & Holiday Course Regulation from Mr. Nagano.
　　　A postal from Mr. Honma.
　　　A copy of Pictorial War Report from home.

1隻と巡洋艦も破壊されたと公式に報じられた。

6月26日日曜　天気　晴にわか雨
　午前中『ポール・パトフ』を読んだ。ハムステッド・カンバセーションの倫理研究所の会合に行った。それは宗教とは関係ない倫理の日曜集会である。彼等は特別な讃美歌があり、子供たちの日曜学校を行っている。

6月27日月曜　天気　晴　寒暖　暖
　午前中『文法書』と『ポール・パトフ』を読んだ。午後と夜は『ポール・パトフ』を読み、パラフレージングに関する課題を書いた。
　トルストイの戦争の悪に関する印象的な宣言が今日のタイムズ紙に掲載された。

6月28日火曜　天気　晴　寒暖　暖
　午前中は日本から来た書状を読んだ。
　パラフレージングに関する課題を清書した。午後レッスンを受けに行った。トルストイ伯爵の「戦争について」をタイムズ紙で読んだ。

Letters from Messrs. Nagaya & Takahashi.
Letters from E.S.S. & Takahashi (stud.).

6月29日水曜　天気　Fair　寒暖　Warm

Read *Grammar* & *Paul Patoff*. Went to see Dr. Ritter who was not at home.

Capture of three important passes – Taling Pass, Matien-ling Pass, & Fuen-chu-ling Pass – forcing the Russians to retreat.

Bought cotton vest & pants & woolen socks.

発信　The Times to Mr. Hojo.
　　　A postal to the Children.
　　　A postal to Mr. Nagano.
　　　A letter to Mr. Ingram.

6月30日木曜　天気　Fair　寒暖　Warm 75°

Read　*Grammar* & *Paul Patoff*.

Went to take lesson.

Wrote exercises with prepositions in sentences.

Two letters for exercise.

発信　A letter to Mr. Melhuish.
受信　A letter from Mr. Melhuish.

7月

7月1日金曜　天気　Fair Rained a little p.m.　寒暖　Cooler 70°

Read　*Grammar* & *Paul Patoff*.

Went to the Yokohama Specie Bank, Bishop's gate str. & received £ 30 & £ 1-18-9.

6月29日水曜　天気　晴　寒暖　暖

『文法書』と『ポール・パトフ』を読んだ。ドクトル・リットルを訪ねたが、不在だった。

3か所の重要な水道［注：地名は不明］を抑えたことで、ロシア軍が退却を余儀なくされた。

綿のチョッキとパンツとウールの靴下を購入した。

6月30日木曜　天気晴　寒暖　暖　75°

『文法書』と『ポール・パトフ』を読んだ。

レッスンを受けに行った。

文中の前置詞に関する課題を書いた。

課題のために2通の書状。

7月

7月1日金曜　天気　晴午後小雨　　寒暖　気温下り70°

『文法書』と『ポール・パトフ』を読んだ。

ビショップゲイトストリートの横浜正金銀行に行って、30ポンドと1ポンド18シリング9ペンスを受け取った。

Bought a hair brush(3'6d), bottle of oil (9d) & a towel (10d).

発信　A postal to Dr. Ritter.
受信　A postal from Mr. Suzuki (Birmingham).
　　　A postal from Mr. Ingram.
　　　A postal from Mr. Nagano.

　　7月2日土曜　天気　Fair Rained occasionally　寒暖　Cool

At 9 in the morning took the train at Paddington & stopped at Reading for some time & changing the train reached Heale at 1/4 before 11. Then in a trap got at Bradfield College 1/2 past 11. Mr. Ingram took me all over the College & also to the sanitarium belonging to the College. Took lunch with masters and students in the dining hall. Left at 2 & got at the station (3 1/2ms walking) at 3, then to Paddington by train, returned home 5.30 p.m. The College has 270 scholars.

発信　A Telegram to Dr. Uchida.
　　　A letter (receipt) to Chyuokinko.
　　　2 postals to home (☐☐on 7th).
受信　A postal from Dr. Uchida.
　　　A letter from Mr. Melhuish.

　　7月3日日曜　天気　Fair　Shower　寒暖　Cool

Went to Hampstead Heath. Caught in a shower, amused to see people sheltering under trees.

After dinner went to Kew gardens. On coming back took electric tram to Shepherd's Bush, went to see Dr. Uchida, in Mornington Avenue, took supper with him. On going there met Mr. Nagano whom I took to Dr. Uchida's. Came home 11 1/2 in the evening.

ヘアブラシ（3シリング6ペンス）、オイル1瓶（9ペンス）タオル1本（10ペンス）を購入した。

7月2日土曜　天気　晴時々雨　寒暖　涼

午前9時にパディントン駅から列車に乗り、レディングに少々止まり、列車を乗り換えてヒールに11時15分前に着いた。それから馬車でブラッドフィールド大学に11時半に到着した。イングラム氏が大学中を案内してくれて、さらに大学附属のサナトリウムにも連れて行ってくれた。ダイニング・ホールで大学院生と学部生たちと昼食を共にした。2時に大学を出て3.5マイル歩いて3時に駅に着き、それから列車でパディントンに戻り5時半に帰宅した。大学には270名の学者がいる。

7月3日日曜　天気　晴にわか雨　寒暖　涼

ハムステッド・ヒースに行った。にわか雨に降られて、人々が木の下に雨宿りをしているのを見るのも愉快であった。

夕食後キューガーデンに行った。帰路はシェパーズブッシュまで電車に乗って、モーニングトン・アヴェニューの内田博士に会いに行き、夕食を共にした。途中で永野氏に会って、彼を内田博士のところに連れて行った。夜11時半に帰宅した。

7月4日月曜　天気　Fair　寒暖　Cool

Read *Grammar* & *Paul Patoff*.

Took a short walk in the neighbourhood.

Wrote letters in the evening.

発信　A letter to Mr. Melhuish.
　　　A letter to Mr. Ingram.
受信　A postal from Mr. Matsui Keisho.
　　　Asagaodame from Mr. Kobayashi Hikozi.
　　　2 letters & a postcard from home.
　　　A letter from Mr, Wachi & another from Mr. Ibuki.
　　　2 Pictorial reports from Mr. Hojo.
　　　A pictorial report from Seki.

7月5日火曜　天気　Fair　寒暖　Cool 65°+

Read *Grammar* & *Paul Patoff* & finished. Took a short walk in the vicinity.

Wrote letters in the evening.

受信　The Student.
　　　International Club compositions.

7月6日水曜　天気　Fair　寒暖　Warmer 76°

Went to the Crystal Palace. Left home 10 a.m. took train from Victoria station & came home 1/4 before 7 p.m.

Wrote letters in the evening.

発信　A letter to Seki (& Wachi).
　　　A postal to Mr. Hojo.
　　　2 postals to home.

7月4日月曜　天気　晴　寒暖　涼
『文法書』と『ポール・パトフ』を読んだ。
近所を少し散歩した。
夜は書状を認めた。

7月5日火曜　天気　晴　寒暖　涼　65°＋
『文法書』と『ポール・パトフ』を読み、読了した。近所を少し散歩した。
　夜は書状を認めた。

7月6日水曜　天気　晴　寒暖　気温上り76°
水晶宮に行った。家を10時に出て、ヴィクトリア駅から列車に乗り、7時15分前に帰宅した。
　夜は書状を認めた。

受信　A letter from Mr. Melhuist.

7月7日木曜　天気　Cloudy　寒暖　Close 67°
　　Wrote exercises in the morning. Reads *Grammars*. Went to take lesson.

発信　A letter to home.
　　　A postalto home.
　　　A postal to Mr. Burnside.
　　　A postal to Mr. Nagano.

7月8日金曜　天気　Fair　寒暖　Close
　　Read *grammars*. Invited to dinner by Capt. Lacock South Kensington. Stayed overnight at Mr. Nagano's lodging.

発信　A postal to Mr. Nagaya.
受信　A postal from Mr. Nagano.
　　　A postal from Mr. Hara.

7月9日土曜　寒暖　80°
　　Stayed till 1 p.m. at Mr. Nagano's. Went to Junior United Service Club, Charles Str. to take lunch with Capt. Lacock. Went to Exeter Hall to attend monthly meeting. Met there Mr. Yamamuro & 5 other Salvationists. Dr. Uchida called & left message.
　　Hot.

発信　2 postals to home (wrote at Mr. Nagano's).

7月10日日曜　天気　Fair　寒暖　82° 2 p.m.
　　Went to Hampstead Heath in the morning. Mrs. Moss returned after

7月7日木曜　天気　曇　寒暖　蒸し暑し67°
午前中課題を書いた。『文法書』を読んだ。レッスンを受けに行った。

7月8日金曜　天気　晴　寒暖　蒸し暑し
『文法書』を読んだ。サウス・ケンジントンのラコック大尉に夕食に招かれた。永野氏の下宿に一泊した。

7月9日土曜　寒暖　80°
永野氏のところに午後１時迄滞在した。ラコック大尉と昼食を取るためにチャールズ・ストリートのジュニア・ユナイテッド・サービス・クラブ［注：軍人のクラブ］に行った。月例会に出席するためにエクセター・ホールに行った。そこでヤマムロ氏及び５人の救世軍軍人に会った。内田博士が来訪し、メッセージを残していた。
　暑い。

7月10日日曜　天気　晴　寒暖　午後２時82°
午前中ハムステッド・ヒースに行った。モス夫人は旅行で何週間も留守

several weeks' absence for a trip. Read *grammar*.

　　Hot in the afternoon, cool toward the evening.

発信　A letter to Dr. Uchida.
　　　A letter to Herr Toda (Berlin).

　　7月11日月曜　天気　Fair　寒暖　78° 10 a.m. 75° 2 p.m.

　　Read *grammar* &c. Hot, but cool wind. Capture of Kai ping reported & confirmed afterward.

発信　A postal to Mr. Nagano.
受信　A postal from Mr. Nagano.

　　7月12日火曜　天気　Fair Shower in the evening　寒暖　78° + 2 p.m.

　　Wrote a composition. Went to take lesson.
　　Hot, windy. Read *grammar* & c.
　　Bought two ties & a pair of sock.

受信　A letter & the prospectus of Bradfield College from Mr. Ingram.

　　7月13日水曜　天気　Fair　寒暖　78°

　　Read *Grammar* &c. Cool breeze. Went to the Lacock's, South Kensington, for the return call; they were not at home.

発信　A postal to Mr. Nagano.
　　　A postal to Mr. Ingram.
受信　A postal from Mr. Nagano.

　　7月14日木曜　天気　Fair　寒暖　82°

　　Read *grammar* & c. Wrote a composition in the form of a

にしていたが帰宅していた。『文法書』を読んだ。
　午後は暑かったが、夜になるにつれて涼しくなった。

　7月11日月曜　天気　晴　寒暖　午前10時78°　午後2時75°
　『文法書』その他を読んだ。暑いが涼しい風が吹いている。蓋平の占領が報じられ、その後確認された。

　7月12日火曜　天気　晴 夕方にわか雨　寒暖　午後2時78°強
　英作文をした。レッスンを受けに行った。
暑いが風がある。『文法書』その他を読んだ。
ネクタイを2本と靴下1足を購入した。

　7月13日水曜　天気　晴　寒暖　78°
　『文法書』その他を読んだ。涼しい風が吹いている。訪問の返礼にサウスケンジントンのラコック家を訪ねたが、不在だった。

　7月14日木曜　天気　晴　寒暖　82°
　『文法書』その他を読んだ。2人の友人間の会話の形式で英作文をした。

conversation between two friends. Went to take lesson.
Cool breeze.

受信　A letter from home.
A letter from Mr. Midzuashi.

7月15日金曜　天気　Fair　寒暖　85°

Read *grammar* &c. Went to the Maxwells. Breezy, but very hot. Capture of Yingkow reported. Cool breeze towards evening.

7月16日土曜　天気　Fair　寒暖　80° 2 p.m. 80° 6 p.m.

Read *grammar* &c. Mr. Burnside failed to come. Very hot. Cool breeze in the evening.

7月17日日曜　天気　Fair　寒暖　81° 2 p.m. 85° 6 p.m.

Took walk on Hampstead Heath.

Read *grammar* & c. Went to the Vienna Café to see Dr. Ritter, and found that he went home (Vienna) a fortnight since. Very close all day till late in the evening.

7月18日月曜　天気　Fair　寒暖　78°

Went to the City & ordered a thinner suit & a pair of trousers at 3-2,6 for both (18/6 Trous, £ 2-4-0 Suit) at Chappell's; bought a straw hat 3' 6d & a copy of Amateur Photographer 1s. Breezy, cool & fresh.

受信　A letter from International Club.

7月19日火曜　天気　Fair　寒暖　79°

Wrote an exercising on Paraphrasing Shelly's "Age of Pericles." Went

レッスンを受けに行った。
　風が涼しい。

　7月15日金曜　天気　晴　寒暖　85°
『文法書』その他を読んだ。マックスウェル家に行った。風はあるが、とても暑い。
　営口市の占領が報じられた。夜になるにつれて涼しい風が吹いている。

　7月16日土曜　天気　晴　寒暖　午後2時80°　午後6時80°
『文法書』その他を読んだ。バーンサイド氏は来なかった。とても暑い。夜には涼しい風が吹いた。

　7月17日日曜　天気　晴　寒暖　午後2時81°　午後6時85°
　ハムステッド・ヒースを散歩した。
『文法書』その他を読んだ。ドクトル・リットルに会いにヴィエナ・カフェに行ったが、彼は2週間前に故郷（ウィーン）に帰ったことがわかった。夜遅くなるまで一日中蒸し暑かった。

　7月18日月曜　天気　晴　寒暖　78°
　シティに行き、チャペルで薄いスーツとズボンを両方で3ポンド2シリング6ペンスでオーダーした（ズボン18シリング6ペンス、スーツは2ポンド4シリング）。麦わら帽子を3シリング6ペンス、『アマチュア・フォトグラファ』1冊1シリングで購入した。風があり、涼しく、爽快である。

　7月19日火曜　天気　晴　寒暖　79°
　シェリーの『ペリクレス時代』をパラフレーズする課題を書いた。レッ

to take lesson. Wrote letters. Cool breeze; fresh.

受信　A letter from Mr. Burnside.

　７月20日水曜　天気　Fair　寒暖　78°
Went to the City & tried on the suit at Chappell's.
Wrote a composition on the Love of nature by the people of Japan. Wrote letters.

　７月21日木曜　天気　Fair　寒暖　78°
Copied the composition. Went to take lesson.
Vladivostok Fleet reported to have passed the Tsugaru strait & steamed in south eastern direction. English government lodged a strong worded protest at St. Petersburg government against the Russian Capture of a P. O. liner, the Malacca, in the Red Sea.

　７月22日金曜　天気　Fair　寒暖　Cool 73°
Bought a Copy of *Richard II* (2d) at New Oxford Street. Bought Cotton Vest Coat (4/11) at Charles Bakers at Euston Corner. Cotton vest (1/9) & pants (1/9), & 2 pairs of socks (1/0 each) at Tottenham Court Road.
Bought 2 fancy (?) shirts (4/6 & 3/6) at Belsize Park Gardens.
Cool breeze. Read *grammar* & *Anglo-saxon*.

発信　A letter & 3 postals to home.
　　　Sphere to home.
　　　Amateur Photographer to Mr. Obana.
　　　A letter to Mr. Shinmi.
　　　A letter to Mr. Melhuist.

スンを受けに行った。書状を認めた。涼しい風が爽快である。

7月20日水曜　天気　晴　寒暖　78°
シティに行ってチャペルの店でスーツの試着をした。
「日本人の自然に対する愛着」について英作文をした。書状を認めた。

7月21日木曜　天気　晴　寒暖　78°
英作文を清書した。レッスンを受けに行った。
　ウラジオストック艦隊は津軽海峡を通過して、南東の方向へ進んでいると報じられている。英国政府は、ペニンシュラー・アンド・オリエンタル海運会社の定期船「マラッカ号」［注；紅海でロシア巡洋艦によってイギリス船マラッカ号が差し押さえられた事件］が紅海でロシアに抑えられたことに対して、ロシア政府に強い語調で抗議した。

7月22日金曜　天気　晴　寒暖　涼　73°
　ニューオックスフォードストリートで『リチャード2世』（2ペンス）を購入した。ユーストン・コーナーのチャールズ・ベイカーズでコットンのベスト・コートを購入した（4シリング11ペンス）。トッテナム・コート・ロードで、コットン・ベスト（1シリング9ペンス）、パンツ（1シリング9ペンス）、靴下2足（1足1シリング）。
　ベルサイズ・パーク・ガーデンズで高級な（？）シャツを2枚（4シリング6ペンスと3シリング6ペンス）購入した。
　涼しい風が吹いている。『文法書』と『アングロサクソン』を読んだ。

受信　A letter from Mr. Melhuist.
　　　A package from Chappell &c.

7月23日土曜　天気　Fair　寒暖　78°

Taking 9 1/4 train at Paddington went to Great Marlow, whence in boats to Henley. Took lunch at the Red Lion Hotel. The Company Dr. Horton & 17 others. Came home by 5 1/2 train Henley. Got home 7 1/2 p.m. The weather fair & cool. Enjoyed much.

Thanks to Mr. Maxwell who paid for everything for the party. Mr. Lorenty left for Bulgaria. Mr. Kemp came to lodge.

7月24日日曜　天気　Fair　寒暖　78°

Went to Lyndhurst Church, then to Hampstead Heath in the morning.
Went to tea at Mr. Melhuist East Sheen, on going took train Hampstead Heath Station —Richmond, on coming home took buses.

7月25日月曜　天気　Shower　寒暖　72°1/2

Read *grammar* & c. Called on Mrs. Maxwell. A Heavy thunderstorm in the afternoon. The Underground line flooded. Borrowed 2 vols of The Berlitz Method from Mr. Kemp.

受信　2 letters & 3 postals from home.
　　　A letter from Mr. Hashimoto (Iwakuni).

7月26日火曜　天気　Cloudy　寒暖　73°

Wrote exercises. Went to take lesson. Paid £ 1-5-0 for 10 lessons (Jun. 23 – Jul 26).

Read *Grammar* & c.

7月23日土曜　天気　晴　寒暖　78°
　パディントンから9時15分の列車に乗ってグレイト・マーローに行き、そこから船でヘンリーへ行った。レッドライオンホテルで昼食を取った。一行はホートン博士と他17名である。ヘンリーを5時半に出る列車に乗り、午後7時半に帰宅した。天候がよく涼しかった。大変楽しかった。
　マックスウェル氏が一行のお金を全て払ってくれて感謝している。ロレンティ氏がブルガリアに発った。ケンプ氏が下宿することになった。

7月24日日曜　天気　晴　寒暖　78°
　午前中はリンドハースト教会に行って、それからハムステッド・ヒースに行った。
　イースト・シーンのメルヒュイッシュ氏のところへお茶に行き、行きはハムステッド・ヒース駅からリッチモンドまで列車に乗って、帰りはバスに乗った。

7月25日月曜　天気　にわか雨　寒暖　72°半
　『文法書』その他を読んだ。マックスウェル夫人を訪問した。午後はひどい雷雨となった。地下鉄が冠水した。ベルリッツ・メソッドを2冊ケンプ氏から借りた。

7月26日火曜　天気　曇　寒暖　73°
　課題を書いた。レッスンを受けに行った。1ポンド5シリングを10回分（6月23日〜7月26日）のレッスン代として支払った。
　『文法書』その他を読んだ。

ロンドン滞在日記　153

Reported New Chang entered by the Japanese.

7月27日水曜　天気 Cloudy　寒暖　Cool

Went to Parmiter's School, Approach Rd. Cambridge Heath N. E. Met Mr. W. S. Daddo, the Second Master. No lesson going on. The last day of the term. Prizes to be given on the next day. The Malacca released.

Bought The *Heart of Rom*e by Marion Crawford. (3'). Went to Regent Str. to inquire about the National Review. Owner changed, nothing to be ascertained. Read *grammar* &c. Had lunch at Exeter Hall Dining Room.

発信　Postals to Nakanome, Nagano, Hirata (Oxford).

7月28日木曜　天気　Fair　寒暖　Cool 69°

Read *Grammar* & c.

Went to Parmiter's School to attend the Speech Day. Prizes distributed by the Right Rev. and Right Hon. The Lord Bishop of London (Mr. Ingram?). Came home 11 1/2 p.m.

Mr. De Plehve, the Russian minister of Interior assassinated with bomb in St. Petersburgh.

Tashi Chao occupied by the Japanese Army. Gen Kuropatkim reported wounded.

発信　A postal to home.
受信　A letter from Mr. Nagano.
　　　A postal from Mr. Burnside.

7月29日金曜　天気　Cloudy　寒暖　76°

Read *grammar* &c.

General assault of Port Arthur reported to have begun.

New Changは日本軍よって陥落させられたと報じられている。

7月27日水曜　天気曇　寒暖　涼
ケンブリッジヒースN.E.のアプローチロードにあるパルミターズ・スクールを見学に行った。教頭のW.S.ダドー氏に会った。授業は行われていなかった。学期の最終日であった。賞は翌日授与されることになっている。マラッカ号は解放された。

マリオン・クロフォード著『ローマのハート』を購入した（3シリング）。ナショナル・リビューについて問い合わせにリージェント・ストリートに行った。オーナーが代わっていて何も確認できなかった。『文法書』その他を読んだ。エクセター・ホールのダイニング・ホールで昼食を取った。

7月28日木曜　天気　晴　寒暖　涼　69°
『文法書』その他を読んだ。
スピーチ・デイに出席するためにパルミターズスクールを訪ねた。賞は尊師であるロンドンの主教（イングラム氏？）によって授与された。午後11時半帰宅。

ロシアの内相デプレーブ氏がサンクト・ペテルブルグで爆弾により暗殺された。

Tashi Chaoが日本軍によって占領された。クロパトキン将軍が負傷したと報道されている。

7月29日金曜　天気　曇　寒暖　76°
『文法書』その他を読んだ。
旅順の総攻撃が始まったと報じられている。

発信　A letter to Mr. Daddo.
　　　A letter toMr. Melhuist.
受信　A postal from Herr Toda.
　　　A postal from Mr. Suzuki (Liverpool).

7月30日土曜　天気　Cloudy　寒暖　82°
Mr. Burnside came to give lesson.
Vladivostok Fleet reported chased by Japanese cruisers in the Pacific.
Read *grammar* & c.
A shower in the afternoon. Weather close.
Dasy and Lily go to Hasting.

受信　A postal from Mr. Hirata.

7月31日日曜　天気　Fair　寒暖　76°
Attended Lyndhurst church. Took bath.
Went to Miss Maxwell's to tea. Attended an evening service in Lyndhurst church.
Vladivostok Fleet reported passed the Strait of Tsugaru bound homeward.

8月

8月1日月曜　天気　Fair　寒暖　79°
Bank Holiday (1st Monday of August)
Went to Windsor with Herr Webber & Herr Kempe, saw the Castle & went to Eton on the other side of the Thames saw the College buildings. Went out in a boat on the river. Came home 7 1/2 p.m. Expenditure 5'10d.

7月30日土曜　天気　曇　寒暖　82°
バーンサイド氏がレッスンに来訪。
ウラジオストック艦隊は太平洋において日本の巡洋艦に追尾されたと報じられる。
『文法書』その他を読んだ。
午後にわか雨が降った。蒸し暑い。
デイジーとリリーはヘイスティングに行く。

7月31日日曜　天気　晴　寒暖　76°
リンドハースト教会に出席した。入浴した。
マックスウェル嬢宅へお茶に行った。リンドハースト教会に夜の礼拝に行った。
ウラジオストック艦隊は津軽海峡を通ってロシアの方向に向かっていると報じられる。

8月

8月1日月曜　天気　晴　寒暖　79°
バンク・ホリデー（8月の第1月曜日）。
ウェバー氏とケンプ氏と一緒にウィンザーに行き、城を見て、テームズ川の対岸にあるイートンを訪れ、大学の建物を見た。ボートに乗って川に出た。午後7時半に帰宅。支出は5シリング10ペンス。
ロシアの将軍ケラーの戦死が報じられる。旅順における熾烈な戦闘の報

A Russian general Keller reported killed. Reports of a severe battle in Port Arthur continued coming, the report of its capture expected every moment. The Capture was reported but not confirmed .

発信　A postal to home (posted at Windsor).
受信　A letter from Monbusho.
　　　War Pictures from home.
　　　War Pictures fromMr. Obana.

8月2日火曜　天気　Fair　寒暖　82°
Wrote letters. Read Anglosaxon book &c.
Miss Lily & Mrs. Moss came home.

発信　A letter & 2 postals to home.
　　　Daily Graphic to home.
　　　Daily Graphic to Mr. Hojo.
　　　A postal to Mr. Hojo.

8月3日水曜　天気　Fair　寒暖　88° 2p.m.
Read the *Heart of Rome*.

Went out driving with Mrs. Maxwell to Hendan & saw the Church built in the 11th century. Very hot, 132° in the sun. Hottest day recorded.

"For hours & hours & hours the ruthless sun kept it up-- keen on breaking records & enticing apoplexy" .

発信　A letter to Mr. Hashimoto (Iwakuni).

8月4日木曜　天気　Fair　Shower afternoon　寒暖　91°
Read the *Heart of Rome* &c.

Went to see Mrs. Maxwell who sent a note to call. She spoke of a

道が次々となされており、旅順の占領が今か今かと待たれる。占領は報じられてはいるが、確認されていない。

8月2日火曜　天気　晴　寒暖　82°
書状を認めた。アングロサクソンの本その他を読んだ。
リリー嬢とモス夫人が帰って来た。

8月3日水曜　天気　晴　寒暖　午後2時88°
『ローマのハート』を読んだ。
マックスウェル夫人とヘンダンにドライブして、11世紀に建設された教会を見た。大変暑く、日向は132度あった。史上最高気温の日であった。
「何時間も何時間も無慈悲な太陽は照り続け、記録を破り、卒中を引き起こすのに夢中になった。」

8月4日木曜　天気　晴午後にわか雨　寒暖　91°
『ローマのハート』他を読んだ。
マックスウェル夫人が招いてくれたので訪問した。彼女はフィンチリー

boarding house in Finchley Road.

　　Disagreeably hot. The hottest day (91°) & fairly breaks the preceding record. Fresh after a shower late in the afternoon.

発信　A letter to Dr. Ritter (Wien).
　　　A postals to Toda, Nakanome, Kodama (New Castle).
受信　A note from Mrs. Maxwell.

　8月5日金曜　天気　Fair　寒暖　78°
　　Read *grammar* &c. Finished *the Heart of Rome*.
　　Had a drive with the Maxwells to Hyde Park & St. James Park &c.
　　Went to see the rooms at Mrs. Giles at Broadhurst Gardens, Finchley Road.
　　Hot, but fresh.

発信　A postal to Mr. Hirata.
受信　A note from Mrs. Maxwell.

　8月6日土曜天気　Fair　寒暖　72°
　　Read *grammar* &c. Mr. Burnside came to give a lesson. Paid him £ 1-1-0. Windy & cool.

受信　A letter from home.
　　　A letter fro Mr. Nagaya.
　　　2 postals from home.
　　　A postal from Mr. Hirata.
　　　A report from Yok. Spec. Bank (London).

　8月7日日曜　天気　Fair　寒暖　71°
　　Attended Dr. Horton's Church. Took walk on the Heath.

ロードの下宿屋の話をした。
　不快なほど暑い。最も暑い日（91度）で前の記録をかなり更新した。午後遅い時間にわか雨が降りさわやかになった。

　　8月5日金曜　天気　晴　寒暖　78°
『文法書』その他を読んだ。『ローマのハート』を読了した。
マックスウェル家と一緒にハイド・パークやセントジェイムス・パークなどにドライブした。
　フィンチリ・ロードのブロードハーストガーデンズのジャイルズ夫人のところに部屋を見に行った。
　暑いがさわやかである。

　　8月6日土曜天気　晴　寒暖　72°
『文法書』その他を読んだ。バーンサイド氏がレッスンに来訪した。彼に1ポンド1シリングを払った。風があって涼しい。

　　8月7日日曜　天気　晴　寒暖　71°
ホートン博士の教会に出席した。ヒースを散歩した。

Went to see Maxwells. Had tea & supper.
Fresh & cool.

発信　Postals to Mr. Nagano & Mr. Hirata.
　　　A letter to the Yok. Spce. Bank.［注：横浜正金銀行］

8月8日月曜　天気　Fair　寒暖　73°

Read *grammar* &c. Took a walk to Primrose Hill.
Mr. Mimoto called; is going to leave for Japan on the 23rd.
Weather clear. No fresh war news forth coming.

発信　A postal to Mr. Nagano.
受信　The Student.
　　　A postal from Mr. Nagano.

8月9日火曜　天気　Fair　寒暖　79°

Took a walk to Primrose Hill in the morning, bought a chair ticket, available for a day in Primrose Hill, Regent's Park & Hyde Park.

In the evening went to London University (Imperial Institute) south Kensington, to attend Prof. Griffin's lecture on Browning, & Prof. Lipman's (?) reading from Hern's Kokoro.

Came home late. Went to Henry Sotheran & co, Piccadilly, and to see Edward Arnold, Bond St. the latter of whom was away from London.

発信　A postal to Mr. Kodama.
受信　A postal from Mr. Hirata.

8月10日水曜　天気　Fair　寒暖　70° 2 p.m.

Went to the Yokohama Specie Bank Bishopsgate, & received £ 29-15-4. Went to Japanese Consulate 1 Broad St. Place, Finsbury Circus, &

マックスウェル家に行った。お茶と夕食を頂いた。
さわやかで涼しい。

8月8日月曜　天気　晴　寒暖　73°
『文法書』その他を読んだ。プリムローズ・ヒルに散歩に行った。
三本氏来訪。彼は23日に帰国予定。
天候は晴天。新たな戦争のニュースはない。

8月9日火曜　天気　晴　寒暖　79°
　午前中はプリムローズ・ヒルに散歩に行き、プリムローズ・ヒル、リージェンツ・パーク、ハイドパークで、1日使える椅子のチケットを買った。
　夜はサウス・ケンジントンのロンドン大学（インペリアル・インスティチュート）に行き、グリフィン教授のブラウニングについての講義と、リップマン（？）教授のハーンの「心」の講読に出席した。
　遅く帰宅した。ピカデリーのヘンリー・サザラン社、それからボンドストリートのエドワード・アーノルドに会いに行った。後者はロンドンを留守にしていた。

8月10日水曜　天気　晴　寒暖　午後2時70°
　ビショップスゲイトの横浜正金銀行に行って、29ポンド15シリング4ペンス受け取った。フィンズベリー・サーカスのブロードセントプレイス1

received a postal from Monbusho.

Wrote letters in the evening.

8月11日木曜　天気　Rain　寒暖　64° 2 p.m.

Port Arthur Fleet reported escaped!

Read *grammar* & c.

Very cool, almost chilly.

受信　A postal from Kobayashi, Nikko.

　　　A postal from Mr. Kodama, New Castle on Tyne.

8月12日金曜　天気　Fair　寒暖　68°

Bought ribbons of Barnes & co, Finchley Road.

A Naval battle off Port Arthur reported, result unknown.

Read *Grammar* & c.

Port Arthur Fleet battered & dispersed by Admiral Togo.

発信　A letter to home.

　　　A letter to Mr. Nagaya.

　　　National Gallery Catalogue to Mr. Hojo.

　　　Sphere & Story books to home.

受信　A postal from Mr. Hara.

8月13日土曜　天気　Fair　寒暖　72°

Read *grammar* &c.

Went to Mr. Buxton's, Widbury, Ware.

Train: Liverpool st. Station － Ware.

Party: Mr. & Mrs. Watanabe (Chiharu), Mr. Hara& Mr. Tanaka.

The Buxton is a well-known family in England. The grandfather of Mr. Buxton, Sir T. Buxton is well-known for his devoted work of the

番の日本領事館に行って、文部省からの葉書を受け取った。
　夜は書状を認めた。

8月11日木曜　天気　雨　寒暖　午後2時64°
旅順の艦隊が逃げたと報じられている。
『文法書』その他を読んだ。
とても涼しく、寒いと言ってもいいくらいだ。

8月12日金曜　天気　晴　寒暖　68°
フィンチリーロードのバーンズ社のリボンを購入した。
旅順沖の海戦が報じられているが、結果は不明である。
『文法書』その他を読んだ。
旅順艦隊は東郷提督に打ちのめされ散り散りに逃げた。

8月13日土曜　天気　晴　寒暖　72°
『文法書』その他を読んだ。
ウェアのウィドベリーのバクストン氏の邸宅に行った。
　列車：リバプール・ストリート駅からウェアまで。
　一行：ワタナベ（チハル）夫妻、ハラ氏、タナカ氏。
バクストン家は英国ではよく知られた家系である。バクストン氏の祖父、サー・T・バクストンは、奴隷解放に献身的に取り組んだことで有名であ

emancipation of slaves. His father Sir Buxton (85 years old) lives near him. He has a very large estate & is very rich.

受信　Shirokane Gakuho. 2

8月14日日曜　天気　Stormy　寒暖　72°

Attended Dr. Horton's Church. Invited by Dr. Horton to lunch on next Wednesday. Put clothes into the Kori.

Mr. & Mrs. Watanabe & Mr. Hara called in the afternoon; had tea; took walk to Hampstead Heath & to Highgate Hill.

One of the Vladivostok Fleet reported sunk by Kamimura.

8月15日月曜　天気　Fair　寒暖　69°

Had a visit from Mr. Nagano, had lunch together, took a walk to Parliament Hill.

発信　A postal to Mr. Mimoto.
　　　A postal to Mr. Hirata.
受信　The Student.

8月16日火曜　天気　Fair　寒暖　68°

Went to King's Cross station & made an inquiry.

Took the luggage to Mr. Mimoto's (1 Trunk, 1 Covered basket, 1 hatbox, 1 Washi bag (books); stayed till after dinner (Japanese food).

Handed a small parcel to Mr. Mimoto to take it to Japan.

Came home late in the evening.

8月17日水曜　天気　Rain　寒暖　62°

Wrote letters.

る。彼の父のサー・バクストン（85歳）が近くに住んでいる。彼は広大な土地を持ち、大変裕福である。

　　8月14日日曜　天気　嵐　寒暖　72°
　ホートン博士の教会に出席した。ホートン博士に水曜日の昼食に招かれた。衣類を行李に入れた。
　ワタナベ夫妻とハラ氏が午後来訪した。お茶を飲み、ハムステッド・ヒースとハイゲイト・ヒルに散歩した。
　ウラジオストック艦隊の1隻が上村［注：彦之丞。日露戦争当時第二艦隊司令長官］に沈没させられたと報じられた。

　　8月15日月曜　天気　晴　寒暖　69°
　永野氏が来訪し、昼食を共にし、パーラメント・ヒルに散歩に行った。

　　8月16日火曜　天気　晴　寒暖　68°
　キングス・クロス駅に行って問い合わせをした。
　荷物を三本氏のところに持って行った（トランク1つ、蓋付きかご1つ、帽子箱1つ、和紙袋〔書籍〕）。夕食（日本食）の後まで滞在した。
　日本に持って帰ってもらうように三本氏に小さな包を渡した。
　夜遅く帰宅。

　　8月17日水曜　天気　雨　寒暖　62°
　書状を認めた。

Invited by Dr. Horton to lunch.
Had hair cut. Took bath.

発信　A postal to Mr. Kodama.
受信　A letter from Monbusho.
　　　Cheque from Chyuokinko
　　　A letter from Mr. Nagano.

　8月18日木曜　天気　Fair a.m. Rain p.m.　寒暖　65°
Leave London for New Castle-on-Tyne.

Taking the train from King's Cross at 10:50 a.m. reached at New Castle-on-Tyne at 5:25 p.m.

Lodging － 72, Gloucester st. (the same house where Mr. Kodama stays).

Met Mr. Kodama in the street & went together to the lodging.

In the evening took a walk to the City which is the busiest part of the place.

発信　A letter to home.
　　　A postal to Monbusho.
　　　Receipt to Chyuokinko.
　　　A postal to Mr. Hara.

　8月19日金曜　天気　Cloudy some rain　寒暖　57°
Newcastle-on-Tyne

Went out to see the place. Bought some pictorial Postcards. The weather chilly.

発信　A postal to Mr. Mimoto.
　　　A postal toWebber.

ホートン博士に昼食に招かれた。
散髪をした。入浴した。

8月18日木曜　天気　午前晴、午後雨　寒暖　65°
ロンドンを発ち、ニューカッスルオンタインへ向かった。
キングスクロス駅から午前10時50分に列車に乗り、ニューカッスルオンタインに午後5時25分に着いた。
宿は、グロースターストリート72番（コダマ氏が泊まっている宿と同じところ）。
通りでコダマ氏に会って、一緒に宿に行った。
夜はここの最もにぎやかな地域であるシティを散歩した。

8月19日金曜　天気　曇少雨　寒暖　57°
ニューカッスルオンタイン
街を見に出かけた。絵葉書を何枚か買った。
肌寒い。

A postal to Suzuki.

A postal toFlory.

受信　A letter from Mr. Hirata, Oxford.

8月20日土曜　天気　Cloudy　寒暖　65°

Newcastle-on-Tyne

Visited Jesmond Dene. This was formerly the private residence of late Lord Armstrong. It was presented to the City as a public park after his death. A bridge over the low ground in front of the park is called Armstrong bridge.

Took a walk to the City in the evening.

発信　A postal to home.

8月21日日曜　天気　Fair　寒暖　62°

Newcastle-on-Tyne

Visited Saltwell Park in Gateshead which is the name given to the district on the left banks of the Tyne.

The Novik reported (officially) sunk, near Korsakoff.

8月22日月曜　天気　Rain　寒暖　53°

Newcastle-on-Tyne

Visited the National History museum.

Mr. Hirayama arrived from London.

発信　A postal to Florie.
受信　2 letters 3 postcards & war pictures from home.

A letter from Akidzuki.

A letter from Mr. Sasao.

A postal from Mr. Tawara.

8月20日土曜　天気　曇　寒暖　65°
ニューカッスルオンタイン
　ジェスモンド・デーンを訪れた。ここはもとは故アームストロング卿の個人の邸宅であった。彼の死後公共の公園としてシティに寄贈された。公園の前の低地にかかる橋はアームストロング・ブリッジと呼ばれる。
　夜シティに散歩に行った。

8月21日日曜　天気　晴　寒暖　62°
ニューカッスルオンタイン
　ゲイツヘッドのソルトウェル公園を訪れた。ゲイツヘッドというのは、タイン川左岸の地域につけられた名前である。
　ノーヴィーク号がコルサコフの近くで沈没したと報じられた（公式に）。

8月22日月曜　天気　雨　寒暖　53°
ニューカッスルオンタイン
　国立自然史博物館を訪れた。
　ヒラヤマ氏がロンドンから到着した。

8月23日火曜　寒暖　62°
Newcastle-on-Tyne
Visited Jesmond Dene & Armstrong Park with Mr. Hirayama. Went & saw Stephenson's first locomotion engine in the station.

受信　A postal from Mr. Suzuki.

8月24日水曜　寒暖　63°
Newcastle-on-Tyne
Visited the Armstrong Ordinance Workshop & Dock yard & saw the Japanese man of war (Kashima) being built. This gigantic concern is one of the largest establishments of its kind in the world & one of the sights of Newcastle, & extends for a mile & 1/4 along the bank of the river (Tyne).

発信　M.S. to Mrs. Flint.
受信　A postal from Florie.

8月25日木曜　天気　Fair　寒暖　63°
Newcastle-on-Tyne
Visited Gosforth Park.
Sebastpol reported damaged by a mine. Askald & Grozovoi reported disarmed in Shanghai by the order of the Tzar.

発信　A letter & Sphere to home.

8月26日金曜　天気　Fair　寒暖　63°
Ncle
Went to the central station to meet Mr. Suzuki who arrived at 12 from Carlisle.

8月23日火曜　寒暖　62°
ニューカッスルオンタイン
　ヒラヤマ氏と共にジェスモンド・ディーンとアームストロング公園を訪れた。
　スティーブンソンの第1号の蒸気機関車のエンジンを見に行った。

8月24日水曜　寒暖　63°
ニューカッスルオンタイン
　アームストロング・オーディナンス工場と海軍工廠を見て、日本の戦艦（鹿島）が建造されているところを見た。この巨大な工場は世界でも最大のものの一つで、ニューカッスルの見ものの一つで、1.25マイルに渡って（タインの）川岸に続いている。

8月25日木曜　天気　晴　寒暖　63°
ニューカッスルオンタイン
　ゴスフォース公園を訪れた。
　セバストポリが水雷で破壊されたと報じられた。アスカルドとグロゾボイはロシア皇帝の命令により上海で武装解除したと報じられた。

8月26日金曜　天気　晴　寒暖　63°
ニューカッスルオンタイン
　カーライルから12時に着く鈴木氏を迎えにセントラル駅に行った。エンパイヤ（ミュージックホール）に行った。

Went to the Empire (Music Hall).

Two Russian destroyers in Port Arthur reported struck the mines & one of them sunk.

発信　A postal to home.
　　　A postal to Mr. Sasao.
　　　A postal to Nagaya.
　　　A postal to Hirata (Oxford).
　　　A postal to Nagano (Channel ids).
　　　A postal to Hojo.
　　　A postal to the Eng. Spk. Society.
受信　A postal from Mr. Suzuki (Carlisle).

8月27日土曜　天気　Fair　寒暖　66°

Ncle

Visited the Saltwell Park &Leazes Park.

Had pictures in group taken by Mr. Suzuki.

The tower of Port Arthur reported entered by the Japanese army, but not confirmed.

受信　A letter from Mrs. Flint.

8月28日日曜　寒暖　73°

Ncle

Had a picture in group taken by Mr. Kodama.

Went to Tynemouth taking a steamboat from the Swing Bridge down the Tyne on going & the electric train on coming back. Tynemouth is a pretty seaside 8 ms from Newcastle.

The party -- Hirayama, Suzuki, Kodama.

郵便はがき

812-8790

158

料金受取人払郵便

博多北局
承　認

0215

差出有効期間
2020年8月31
日まで
（切手不要）

福岡市博多区
　奈良屋町13番4号

海鳥社営業部 行

通信欄

通信用カード

このはがきを,小社への通信または小社刊行書のご注文にご利用下さい。今後,新刊などのご案内をさせていただきます。ご記入いただいた個人情報は,ご注文をいただいた書籍の発送,お支払いの確認などのご連絡及び小社の新刊案内をお送りするために利用し,その目的以外での利用はいたしません。

新刊案内を ［希望する　希望しない］

〒　　　　　　　　　　☎　　　（　　　）
ご住所

フリガナ
ご氏名　　　　　　　　　　　　　　　　　（　　　歳）

お買い上げの書店名	杉森此馬英国留学日記 明治37年1月1日 - 12月31日

関心をお持ちの分野
歴史, 民俗, 文学, 教育, 思想, 旅行, 自然, その他（　　　）

ご意見, ご感想

購入申込欄

小社出版物は,本状にて直接小社宛にご注文下さるか（郵便振替用紙同封の上直送いたします。送料無料),トーハン,日販,大阪屋栗田,または地方・小出版流通センターの取扱書ということで最寄りの書店にご注文下さい。
なお小社ホームページでもご注文できます。http://www.kaichosha-f.co.jp

書名		冊
書名		冊

旅順の2隻のロシアの駆逐艦が水雷を爆発させ、1隻が沈没したと報じられた。

8月27日土曜　天気　晴　寒暖　66°
ニューカッスルオンタイン
ソルトウェルパークとリーゼスパークを訪ねた。
鈴木氏にグループ写真を撮ってもらった。
旅順のタワーに日本軍が入ったと報じられたが、確認は得られていない。

8月28日日曜　寒暖　73°
ニューカッスルオンタイン
グループ写真をコダマ氏に撮ってもらった。
　行きはスウィングブリッジから蒸気船に乗って川を下りタインマウスに行き、帰りは電気列車で帰って来た。タインマウスはニューカッスルから8マイルのきれいな海岸である。
　一行はヒラヤマ、鈴木、コダマ。

8月29日月曜　天気　Fair　寒暖　81°

Ncle

Went to Durham with Mr. Suzuki & visited the castle & Cathedral, two noted Norman architectures. The cathedral is the largest, most beautiful & best conditioned Norman relics, a building of 12th or 13th century.

Weather fair & warm.

発信　3 postals to home.

8月30日火曜　天気　Fair　寒暖　Warm

Ncle

Nothing particular. Spent whole day in chatting & taking walks.

受信　A postal from Kobayashi (Nikko).
　　　A letter from Mr. Obana.
　　　War picturesr from Mr. Obana.

8月31日水曜　東宮御誕辰　天気　Fair

Ncle

Went to Newburn (4 or 5 ms from N'cle.) & saw a steelwork. Rolling process, very interesting.

受信　A letter from home.
　　　2 postals from Yoshi &Nobu.
　　　A letter from Mr. Hara.
　　　A postal from Mr. Lorenty (Belgiun).

8月29日月曜　天気　晴　寒暖　81°
ニューカッスルオンタイン
　鈴木氏とダーラムへ行き、お城と大聖堂の二つの有名なノルマン人の建築物を訪れた。大聖堂はノルマン人の遺物の中で最大で最も美しく最もよい状態で、12世紀または13世紀の建物である。
　天候はよく、暖かい。

8月30日火曜　天気　晴　寒暖　暖
ニューカッスルオンタイン
　特別なことは何もなかった。終日おしゃべりをしたり、散歩したりした。

8月31日水曜　東宮御誕辰　天気　晴
ニューカッスルオンタイン
　ニューバーン（ニューカッスルオンタインから4か5マイル）に行って、鋼鉄製品を見た。圧延工程は大変興味深い。

9月

9月1日木曜　天気　Fair
Ncle－Edinburgh

Left Newcastle at 12:17 a.m. arrived at Edinburgh 4 p.m. Stayed at New Waverley Hotel. Took walk to different streets. The gardens between Prince st. & the castle very pretty. Scott's monument is erected in the gardens. The Flora Clock is also here. This is the prettiest part in Edinburgh, perhaps in the world as a location of a street. The castle rises in the front of it.

9月2日金曜　天気　Fair rain after
Edinburgh － Glasgow

Climbed Nelson Monument on Calton Hill. Visited the Castle & saw the Banqueting Hall, stale prison.

Mary of Scot's bedroom, Arcade room, St. Mary's Chapel &c, bought some postcards. Visited John Knox's House which is a book stall now, bought some postcards. Went round the city on top of a cable tram. Left Edinburgh at 4 p.m. arrived at Glasgow 5：15 p.m. Lodged at Miss Napier's Caledonian Mansion, near Kelvin Bridge.

Victory at Lioyang reported.

発信　A letter to home (From Edinburgh).
　　　Postals to home, Dr. Ibuka, Mr. Obana (from Edinburgh).

9月3日土曜　天気　Fair
Edinburgh － Glasgow

Mr. Ishida called & visited the botanical garden & West End Park. Called on Mr. Isono & took walk in the street, went to Glasgow Bridge.

9月

9月1日木曜　天気　晴
ニューカッスルオンタイン ── エディンバラ

ニューカッスルを12時17分に発ち、エディンバラに午後4時に着いた。ニューウェイバリーホテルに滞在した。いろいろな通りを散歩した。プリンセスストリートとお城の間の庭園が大変美しい。スコッツモニュメントはその庭園に建てられている。花時計もその庭園にある。ここはエディンバラの中でも最も美しい地区で、おそらく通りという場としては世界でも最も美しいと言える。お城はその前にそびえている。

9月2日金曜　天気　晴後雨
エディンバラ ── グラスゴー

カールトンヒルのネルソンモニュメントに上った。エディンバラ城を訪ね、中の宴会場や古臭い牢屋を見た。

スコットランド女王メアリの寝室、アーケイドルーム、セントメアリーチャペル等があり、何枚か絵ハガキを買った。「ジョン・ノックスの家」を訪ねると、そこは今は新聞雑誌スタンドになっており、そこで絵葉書を数枚購入した。ケーブルトラムに乗って市内めぐりをした。エディンバラを午後4時に発ち、グラスゴーに5時15分に着いた。ケルヴィン橋の近くのナピア嬢のカレドニアンマンションに宿を取った。

「遼陽会戦」での勝利が報じられた。

9月3日土曜　天気　晴
エディンバラ ── グラスゴー

イシダ氏来訪し、植物園とウエストエンドパークを訪れた。磯野氏［注：磯野長蔵、当時明治屋副社長］を訪問し、通りを散歩し、グラス

Mr. Saito arrived from Edinburgh. Saw a fancy dress cycle procession. This is to collect fund for the Infirmaries in Glasgow. Glasgow is a large city second in the Kingdom pop. 1,000,000. The shipyard on the Clyde is perhaps largest in the world. Called on Mr. Isono & he called in the evening.

発信　A postal to Flo.
　　　A postal to Mr. Kodama.

９月４日日曜　天気　Shower Rained　寒暖　Cold
Glasgow

Taking a steamer (11 a.m.) at Glasgow Bridge, went down the Clyde & went as far as the Kyles of Bute, & came back to Glasgow 8 p.m. Fare 6/6 including dinner & plain tea. Comparing Prof. Saito, the scenery is less beautiful than the Inland Sea or Noto Bay in Japan. Windy & the sea was rough.

９月５日月曜　天気　Wet
Glasgow

Went out sightseeing. Wrote letters. Went to see Mr. [　　] Queen's Park. The captures of Liao Yang officially reported.

発信　A postal to Mr. Kodama.

９月６日火曜　天気　Shower
Glasgow

Had a call from Mr. Ishida. Went out sightseeing. Wrote letters & postals.

発信　A letter & 4 postals to home.

ゴー橋へ行った。サイトウ氏がエディンバラから着いた。仮装した人々による自転車のパレードを見物した。これはグラスゴーの病院の寄付を集めるためのものである。グラスゴーは百万の人口を持つ英国第2の都市である。クライド川の造船所はおそらく世界最大であろう。磯野氏を訪問し、夜彼が来訪した。

9月4日日曜　天気　にわか雨後雨　寒暖　寒
グラスゴー
午前11時にグラスゴー橋で蒸気船にのり、クライド川を下り、カイルズ・オブ・ブートまで行って、午後8時にグラスゴーまで帰って来た。料金はディナーとティーがついて6シリング6ペンスであった。サイトウ教授は比較して、景色は日本の瀬戸内海や能登湾ほどには美しくないと言った。風が強く海は荒れていた。

9月5日月曜　天気　雨
グラスゴー
観光に出かけた。書状を認めた。クイーンズパークの［氏名不明］氏に会いに行った。遼陽の占領が公式に報じられた。

9月6日火曜　天気　にわか雨
グラスゴー
イシダ氏来訪。観光に出かけた。書状や葉書を認めた。

　　　　Postals to Mr. Hojo, Nagaya, Kiuchi, Hori, & Seki.
受信　A letter from Mr. Hori, K.
　　　A letter from Seki.
　　　A postal from Kiuchi.
　　　Catalogues from Sortheran. Co.
　　　M. S. from International Club.

9月7日水曜　天気　Fair
Glasgow
Mr. Saito left for Liverpool.
　Visited the Municipal Building, £ 1/4 million was spent for the building, it is a beautiful building; Glasgow Cathedral; the public bathing & washing place; the Art gallery & Museum. Took walk to Glasgow Bridge in the evening.

受信　A postal from Mr. Hirata.

9月8日木曜　天気　Rain
Glasgow
Went out sight-seeing.
Sick last night. Well now.
Read the "*Out of the Jaws of Death.*" － a novel.
Called on Mr. Isono, met with Mr. Konokagi from Formosa.

発信　A postal to Mr. Kobayashi.
　　　M.S. to Mr. R. H. Pope.
受信　A letter & a postal from home.
　　　letter & a postal from Mr. Elliott.
　　　letter & a postal from Kurihara.
　　　Postal from Mr. Honma.

9月7日水曜　天気　晴
グラスゴー
サイトウ氏はリバプールへ発った。
　市庁舎を訪れた。25万ポンドがこの建物に費やされ、とても美しい建物である。グラスゴー大聖堂、公衆浴場と洗濯場、アートギャラリー、博物館。夜グラスゴー橋に散歩に行った。

9月8日木曜　天気　雨
グラスゴー
観光に出かけた。
昨夜は体調が悪かった。今日はよくなった。
『死地を脱して』という小説を読んだ。
磯野氏を訪ねた。台湾から来たコノカギ氏と会った。

9月9日金曜　天気　Showery　寒暖　Cold　59°
Glasgow

Went with Mr. Konokagi to Fairfield to see the shipyard where dredgers are made, & the Clyde Bank shipyard where the largest steamer (750ft) was being built. The weather showery.

発信　A postal to Flo.

9月10日土曜　天気　Fair

Left Glasgow at 10:10 a.m. (Caledonian station) reached Manchester (Victoria station) 4:30 p.m. Visited Mr. Kobayashi at Plymouth Grove. Took lodging at 8, Ackart st. Mr. Sekiguchi living in the same house. Took a walk to the City in the evening with Mr. Kobayashi.

受信　A postal from Mr. Nagano.

9月11日日曜　天気　Fair
Manchester

Went to see Mr. Saito in the morning. Went with Mr. Kobayashi to see Baston Bridge in the Manchester Ship Canal.

Mr. Saito called in the evening.

(During August the Manchester Ship Canal receipts were £ 34,524.)

9月12日月曜　天気　Windy Rained a bit
Manchester

Visited Royal Technical Institute in Salford & saw carics printing, weaving & spinning machines.

Mr. Saito left for Birmingham.

Mr. Matsubara called when out.

9月9日金曜　天気　にわか雨　寒暖　寒　59°
グラスゴー
コノカギ氏と共に浚渫船が建造されている造船所を見にフェアフィールドへ、また最大の蒸気船（750フィート）が建造中のクライド河岸の造船所へ行った。にわか雨が降った。

9月10日土曜　天気　晴
グラスゴー（カレドニアン駅）を午前10時10分に発ち、マンチェスター（ヴィクトリア駅）に午後4時30分に着いた。プリマスグローブにコバヤシ氏を訪問。アッカートストリート8番に宿を取った。セキグチ氏が同じ家に住んでいる。夜はコバヤシ氏と街まで散歩した。

9月11日日曜　天気　晴
マンチェスター
午前中サイトウ氏を訪問した。コバヤシ氏と共にマンチェスター船舶運河のバストンブリッジを見学に行った。
　夜サイトウ氏が来訪。
（8月中マンチェスター大型船用運河の収入は34,524ポンドであった。）

9月12日月曜　天気　風強し少雨
マンチェスター
サルフォードの王立科学技術学院を訪問して、印刷機、織機、紡績機を見た。
　サイトウ氏はバーミンガムへ発った。
　留守中に松原氏［注：行一、文部省留学生、化学者］来訪。

9月13日火曜　天気　Fair

Manchester

　Mr. Matsubara called & went with him to see the inside of Owens College & went all over the rooms & the Museum. This is the college where Stanley Jevons & Sir Henry Roscoe were once professors. Took lunch together & visited the Art Gallery in Whitworth Park.

9月14日水曜　天気　Fair

Manchester

　Visited Manchester Technical School & went all over lecture halls & workshops of all departments. This has perhaps the earliest & best appliances in connection with technical education in the world. Visited also Chethan's Hospital or College which has been standing since 13th century; De Quincy is one of the alumini of the school adjoining. Visited the Cathedral, the Free Reference Library, and the Rylands Library, the book of which costed £ 1,000,000 & contains 100,000 vols of books both of which were contributed to the city by Mrs. Ryland in memory of her late husband.

9月15日木曜

Manchester

　Took a walk to Whitworth Park. Went out for sight-seeing. Bought a Manchester-views-album. Called on Mr. Kobayashi who was not in.
発信　Letters to home, Mr. Hojo (& Nagaya).
　Postals to Mr. Homma, Kurihara, Elliott, Lorentz, Tawara, English Speaking Society.

9月16日金曜　天気　Fair　寒暖　Warm

Manchester

9月13日火曜　天気　晴
マンチェスター
　松原氏が来訪し、彼と一緒にオーウェンス大学の中を見学に行き、いろんな部屋を全部見せてもらい、博物館を見学した。ここはスタンリー・ジェヴォンズ［注：経済学者］とサー・ヘンリー・ロスコー［注：化学者］がかつて教授をしていた大学だ。昼食を共にし、ホィットワース・パークのアート・ギャラリーを訪れた。

9月14日水曜　天気　晴
マンチェスター
　マンチェスター科学技術学校を訪問し、すべての学科の講義室と実習室を見学した。ここはおそらく世界で最新最高の科学技術教育関連機器を備えている。13世紀創立のチェザン病院や大学も訪問したが、デ・クインシー［注：評論家］は付属のグラマースクールの同窓生の1人である。大聖堂、無料参考図書館、そしてライランズ図書館に行った。ここは100万ポンド分の10万冊を所蔵する図書館で、図書館・蔵書共に亡き夫の思い出にライランズ夫人が氏に寄贈したものである。

9月15日木曜
マンチェスター
　ホィットワース・パークに散歩に行った。観光に出かけた。マンチェスター・ヴュー・アルバムを購入した。コバヤシ氏を訪ねたが、不在であった。

9月16日金曜　天気　晴　寒暖　暖
マンチェスター

Went to Liverpool 10:30 p.m. saw docks, the Landing Stage, St. George's Hall. Mrs. Herman's birthplace, the house where Hawthorn's "Mrs. Bladgett" lived &c. Came back 6:30.

Called on Mr. Kobayashi & went to the Midland Hotel to see a friend of Mr. Kobayashi's.

発信　A postal to home (From Liverpool).

9月17日土曜　天気　Fair　寒暖　Warm
Manchester

Saw the Life-boat Procession which started at 1 p.m. from Albart Square & went throught the principal streets. The Procession is to receive for the contribution from the crowd which lives the street through which it proceed. The sum received given to the fund for the helping the work of the Life-boat movement. Subscriptions & collections last year amounted to £ 1,900 which was remitted to the central fund. Went to Belle-vue to see fireworks − Bombardment of Port Arthur.

発信　A letter to home.
　　　A postal to Kobayashi.
　　　A postal to Mr. Hirata.

9月18日日曜　天気　Fair　寒暖　Warm
Manchester

Went out for walking to Whitworth Park & the neighbourhood. Went to see Mr. Matsubara to say good bye & took a walk to Birch Lane Park.

発信　Postals to Flo & Mr. Hirata.

10時半にリパプールに行って、ドック、桟橋、セント・ジョージズ・ホールを見学した。ホーソンの「ブラジェット夫人」が住んでいたハーマン夫人の生家等も見た。6時半に帰って来た。
　コバヤシ氏を訪ね、彼の友人に会いに、ミッドランドホテルに行った。

　9月17日土曜　天気　晴　寒暖　暖
　マンチェスター
　午後1時にアルバートスクエアからスタートしメインストリートを行進する救命艇パレードを見た。パレードは通りに住む群衆から寄付を募るためのものである。集まった寄付金は救命艇の運動を助けるための基金に加えられる。昨年の寄付金は1900ポンドに達し、中央基金に送金された。花火を見にベルヴューへ行った。――旅順の爆撃。

　9月18日日曜　天気　晴　寒暖　暖
　マンチェスター
　ホィットワース・パークや周辺に散歩に行った。別れのあいさつに松原氏を訪ね、バーチレーンパークに散歩に行った。

9月19日月曜　天気　Fair
Manchester - Birmingham - Oxford
Left Manchester at 10 a.m. reached Birmingham at 12:20 p.m. visited the museum, & had a round of sight-seeing, took 2:45 train& reached Oxford at 5 p.m. Went to see Mr. Hirata & dined together. Took lodging at 26 Richmond St.

発信　A postal to home (From Birmingham).
　　　Views of Glasgow & Liverpool in books to home(From Manchester).

9月20日火曜　天気　Fair
Oxford
Mr. Hirata called, brought two letters from Japan.
Took a walk with Mr. Hirata, who came to tea after.

受信　A letter from Mr Nagaya & Akidzuki.

9月21日水曜
Oxford
Took a walk to the garden of Worcester College.
Called on Mr. Hirata, had tea together.

発信　A postal to Florie.
　　　A letter to home.

9月19日月曜　天気　晴
マンチェスター ── バーミンガム ── オックスフォード
　午前10時にマンチェスターを発ち、バーミンガムに午後12時20分に着いた。博物館に行き、ひとめぐり観光をし、2時45分の列車に乗って午後5時にオックスフォードに着いた。平田氏に会いに行き、食事を共にした。リッチモンドストリート26番に宿を取った。

9月20日火曜　天気　晴
オックスフォード
平田氏が来訪し、日本からの2通の書状を持って来てくれた。
平田氏と散歩した。後でお茶に来てくれた。

9月21日水曜
オックスフォード
ウスターカレッジの庭園に散歩に行った。
平田氏を訪ね、お茶を共にした

現在のストラットフォード・オン・エイボンのエイボン川

オックスフォード滞在日記

9月22日〜12月31日

オックスフォード大学のラドクリフ・カメラ（図書館の一部、現在）

9月

9月22日木曜　天気　Fair Rain after
Oxford
Changed the lodging – Woolmer House, 46 South-moor Rd.

受信　A letter from Mrs. Walker.

9月23日金曜
Oxford
Took a walk in the neighborhood. Bought a bottle of Bovril.

発信　Postals to Mr. Walker, Mr. Matsubara, Kobayashi, Sekiguchi, Kodama.

9月24日土曜　天気　Showery
Oxford – London
　Left Oxford at 2:12 p.m. reached Paddington at 3:25 & came back to Stanley Gardens 4:15 after absence of a little over five weeks. All well, things look much homelike. Took bath, felt quite refreshed.

発信　A letter to Mr. Miyachi.

9月25日日曜　天気　Fair
London
　Went to Sakura villa, Brondesbury Rd. to bring clothes &c.
　Took a walk with Mr. Kempe, Flo & children to Golden's Hill & had tea in the garden. It was a private residence but after the death of the owner it was given to London County Council & is open to the public. A

9月

9月22日木曜　天気　晴後雨
オックスフォード
下宿を変えた —— サウスムアロード46番ウールマーハウス。

9月23日金曜
オックスフォード。
近隣を散歩した。ボブリル［注：スープ用牛肉エキス］を1瓶購入した。

9月24日土曜　天気　にわか雨
オックスフォード —— ロンドン
　午後2時12分にオックスフォードを発ち、3時25分にパディントンに着き、5週間少しぶりにスタンリーガーデンズに4時15分に帰って来た。万事問題なく、我が家という感じが増している。入浴してさっぱりした。

9月25日日曜　天気　晴
ロンドン
　ブロンデスベリーロードのサクラヴィラに衣類などを取りに行った。
　ケンプ氏とフローと子供たちと一緒にゴールデンズヒルに散歩に行き、庭園でお茶を飲んだ。ここは個人の庭園であったが、所有者の死後、ロンドン州会に寄付され、一般に公開された。大きな果樹園、広大な芝生、花

large orchard, extensive lawn, & flower garden are attached to it & fruits are given to hospitals & similar institutes. Tea is served in the garden & a band plays on Sunday afternoons.

Attended Lyndhurst Church in the evening.

9月26日月曜　天気　Fair　寒暖　60°

Went to the Yokohama Specie Bank, received £ 20. Had a dress & a winter suit ordered at the Chappell. Paid £ 3-8-0 for the suit.

Went to the Japanese consulate& had Oxford address registered.

Paid a visit to Mrs. Maxwell, & to Miss Weber.

発信　Postals to Mr. Suzuki, Nagano, Burnside.
受信　A.M. A letter from home.
　　　A postaltter from home.
　　　A postaltter from Mr. Kobayashi.
　　　P.M. A letter & 2 postals & 1 picture from home.
　　　P.M. A letter from Mr. Ibaraki.
　　　A postal from Mr. Matsubara.
　　　War pictures from Mr. Hojo.
　　　A postal from Miss Totoki.

9月27日火曜　天気　Fair　寒暖　57°

Went to Putney to see Miss Snowdon who is going to leave for Japan on Nov. 1.

Visited Mr. Nagano at Weltje Hammersmith dined together. Came home late in the evening,

受信　A postal from Mr. Nagano.

園が付属しており、果物は病院や類似した施設に配られる。お茶は庭園で供され、日曜の午後は楽団が演奏する。
　夜はリンドハースト教会の礼拝に出席した。

　9月26日月曜　天気　晴　寒暖　60°
　横浜正金銀行に行き、20ポンド受け取った。礼服と冬用上着をチャペルで注文し、上着には3ポンド8シリング払った。
　日本領事館に行き、オックスフォードの住所を登録してもらった。
　マックスウェル夫人及びウェーバー嬢を訪問した。

　9月27日火曜　天気　晴　寒暖　57°
　11月1日に日本へ発つ予定のスノードン嬢に会いにプットニーに行った。
　ウェルチェハンマースミスの永野氏を訪ね、食事をともにした。夜遅く帰宅した。

9月28日水曜　天気　Foggy Fair after　寒暖　66°

Went to Chappell's to try the suit on; went to the Yusenkaisha & saw Mr. Ishii & spoke about the luggage left at Sakura Villa, then to the Mitsui &CO. & saw Mr. Hirayama.

Visited Mr. Oaks, & then called on Mr. Shattack, but was not in.

発信　A letter & 4 postals + "Sphere" to home.
　　　A letter to Mr. Hojo.
　　　Sphere to Mr. Obana.
　　　A letter to Miss Snowdon.

9月29日木曜　天気　Foggy Fair after　寒暖　64°

Spent the whole morning in reading; went to the West End in the afternoon & bought a copy of *First German Course* (1d!) & a copy of *Twelfth Night* (1d!).

Dined at Mrs. Maxwell's in the evening.

受信　A postal from Mr. Burnside.

9月30日金曜　天気　Foggy Fair after　寒暖　62°

Spent the whole day in reading. Went in the evening to see Mr. Suzuki, who has just come back from Cambridge.

Had hair cut, & took bath.

10月

10月1日土曜　天気　Rain　寒暖　62°

London − Oxford

Mr. Suzuki called & took lunch together.

Left for Oxford taking 1.45 train at Paddingon.

9月28日水曜　天気　霧後晴　寒暖　66°

チャペルにスーツの試着に行き、郵船会社に行きイシイ氏に会い、サクラヴィラに残してある荷物について話した。それから三井物産に行ってヒラヤマ氏に会った。

オークス氏を訪問し、それからシャタック氏を訪ねたが不在であった。

9月29日木曜　天気　霧後晴　寒暖　64°

午前中はずっと読書した。午後はウェストエンドに行って、『ドイツ語の初歩』を1冊（1ペニー！）と『十二夜』を」1冊（1ペニー！）購入した。

夜はマックスウェル夫人宅で食事をした。

9月30日金曜　天気　霧後晴　寒暖　62°

終日読書をして過ごした。夜は鈴木氏に会いに行った。鈴木氏はケンブリッジから帰って来たところである。

散髪し、入浴した。

10月

10月1日土曜　天気　雨　寒暖　62°
ロンドン ── オックスフォード
鈴木氏が来訪し昼食を共にした。
パディントンから1時45分の列車に乗り、オックスフォードに向けて出

Arrived at Oxford 3.05. Visited Mr. Hirata who was not in. Mr. Hirata called afterward.

Lodging − Woolmer House, 46, Southmoor Rd. Oxford.

Train Puddington station to Oxford 63ms.

受信　Report from the Yokohama Specie Bank (London).

10月2日日曜　天気　Foul

Spent most of the day in reading.

Called on Mr. Hirata in the afternoon.

10月3日月曜

Mr. Hirata called.

Visited Mrs. Shaw.

Bought *The Sketch Book* (6d) & *Chronicles of Schonberg-Cotta Family* (6d).

発信　A letter to the Yokohama Specie Bank.

A letter to Coak & Co.

A letter to Mr. Nagano.

A postal to Flory.

10月4日火曜

Wrote letters, read *The Sketch Book.*

Mr. Hirata called in the afternoon.

Bought a pair of scissors(3s).

10月5日水曜　天気　Fair Rain after

Oxford − Cardiff

Left Oxford station at 11:25 a.m. for Cardiff, reached 3:25 p.m. Took a lodging at Mr. Jones, 10, Plantagenet St. River-side Cardiff.

発した。

　3時5分オックスフォード着。平田氏を訪ねたが、不在だった。平田氏が後で来訪した。

　下宿はオックスフォード、サウスムアロード46番のウールマーハウスである。

　列車でパディントン駅からオックスフォードまで63マイル。

10月2日日曜　天気　荒天
ほぼ終日本を読んで過ごした。
午後は平田氏を訪問した。

10月3日月曜
平田氏が来訪。
ショー夫人を訪問した。
『スケッチブック』（6ペンス）と『ショーンバーグの年代記 —— コッタ・ファミリー』（6ペンス）を購入した。

10月4日火曜
書状を認め、『スケッチブック』を読んだ。
午後平田氏が来訪した。
鋏を1丁購入（3シリング）。

10月5日水曜　天気　晴後雨
オックスフォード —— カーディフ
オックスフォード駅を午前11時25分にカーディフに向けて発ち、3時25分に着いた。宿をカーディフのリバーサイド、プランタジネットストリー

Visited the Free Library & the Museum (same building) in the evening.

Rained late in the afternoon & the evening.

発信　A letter to home.
　　　A letter to Mr. Nagaya(Mr. K. Hori's & Mr. Kurihara's enclosed).
　　　A postal to Flory.
受信　A letter from Coak & Co.

10月6日木曜　天気　Fair
Cardiff

Went out for sightseeing. Went to Sophia Gardens.

Met Miss Hughes, Mr. Hughes (her brother) & another lady, & Mr. Hirata at the Dorothy Restaurant, St. Mary's Street.

Attended a political meeting at Andrews Hall, where Mr. Lloyd George, Dr. Robertson Nicol, The Hon. Ivor Guest, M.P. & several others made enthusiastic speeches against the Education Bill. Mr. Lloyd George is the leader of the Welsh Party.

発信　2 postals to home.
　　　A postal to Mr. Hojo.
受信　A telegram from Mr. Hirata, Barry.

10月7日金曜　天気　Showery
Cardiff － Barry － Oxford

Went to Barry (leaving Cardiff 9:20 a.m. reached Barry 9:45 a.m.).

Visited Miss Hughes, who was at the station to meet.

Visited a girl's school & a kinder-garten. Saw the ruin of old Barriff? Castle. Left Barry 1 1/2 p.m. reached Oxford 5 1/2 p.m. Stopped at Bristol 40 minutes, strolled in the street near the station.

ト10番ジョーンズ氏のところに取った。
　夜は無料図書館と博物館（同じ建物）を訪れた。
　午後遅くと夜は雨が降った。

10月6日木曜　天気　晴
　カーディフ
　観光に出かけた。ソフィア・ガーデンズに行った。
　ヒューズ嬢、ヒューズ氏（彼女の兄）ともう1人の女性と平田氏とセントメアリーズストリートのドロシー・レストランで会った。
　アンドルーホールで政治集会に参加した。ここではロイド・ジョージ氏とロバートソン・ニコル博士、国会議員アイヴァ・ゲスト閣下と他の人たちが教育法案に反対して熱のこもった演説を行った。ロイド・ジョージ氏はウエルシュ党の党首である。

10月7日金曜　天気　にわか雨
　カーディフ ── バリー ── オックスフォード
　バリーに行った（カーディフを午前9時20分に出てバリーに午前9時45分に着いた。）
　ヒューズ嬢を訪ねた。彼女は出迎えに駅に来てくれた。
　女子学校と幼稚園を訪問した。バリフ（？）城址を見た。バリーを午後1時半に発ち、オックスフォードに午後5時半に着いた。ブリストルで40

発信　A postal to home (posted at Bristol station).
　　　A postal to home (from Oxford).
受信　2 postals from home.
　　　A letter from Rev. Deacon.
　　　A letter from Mr. Nagano.
　　　A letter from Sekiguchi.

10月8日土曜　天気　Fair　Rained　寒暖　Cold
Oxford
Read *Cotta Family*. Had fire for the first time.
Took a walk in the neighbourhood.
Paid for board & washings.

受信　A letter from Miss Hughes.

10月9日日曜　天気　Fair
　Attended a Congregation chapel, George Street.
　Read *Cotta* &c. Called on Mr. Hirata.

10月10日月曜　天気　Foggy
　Russian advance reported.
　Mr. Hirata called, & read *The Sketch Book* (Stratford-on-avon) together.
　Read *Cotta* &c.

10月11日火曜　天気　Fair
　Went to tea at Mr. Hirata's, read *The Sketch book* together.
　Read *Cotta*, wrote letters.

分止まり、駅の近くの通りをぶらぶらした。

10月8日土曜　天気　晴後雨　寒暖　寒
オックスフォード。
『コッタ・ファミリー』を読んだ。初めて暖炉に火を入れた。
近所を散歩した。
下宿代と洗濯代を支払った。

10月9日日曜　天気　晴
ジョージストリートの会衆派チャペルに出席した。
『コッタ』等を読んだ。平田氏を訪問した。

10月10日月曜　天気　霧
ロシアの侵攻が報じられた。
平田氏が来訪し、「スケッチブック（ストラットフォード・オン・エイボン）」を一緒に読んだ。
『コッタ』等を読んだ。

10月11日火曜　天気　晴
平田氏のところにお茶に行き、『スケッチブック』を一緒に読んだ。
『コッタ』を読み、書状を認めた。

10月12日水曜　天気　Fair

　Mr. Hirata called, read together.

　Read *Cotta*, wrote letters.

　A gunboat, Hei-yen reported sunk by a floating mine at Pigeon Bay. 300 lives lost.

　A great battle between Mukden & Lyao-yang reported imminent.

発信　A letter to home.
　　　A letter to Akidzuki.
　　　A letter to Mr. Junker.
　　　A letter to Monbusho.
　　　Papers to Mr. Hojo.

10月13日木曜　天気　Fair

　A big Japanese victory reported. Took a walk to the banks of the Thames.

　Read *Cotta*,&c. Mr. Ota called in the evening.

10月14日金曜　天気　Fair

　Called on Mr. Hirata & read together.

　Kuropatkin reported retreating. Many Russian guns captured.

　Read *Cotta* & c.

10月15日土曜　天気　Fair

　A great battle still going on much favorable to the Japanese. A considerable number of Russians made prisoner; over 30 guns captured. Stassal's wireless telegraphy intercepted by the Japanese. provision & ammunition known to be □□□. The fall of Port Arthur seem to be nearing fast. Visited Prof. Smith (King's Mound).

10月12日水曜　天気　晴
平田氏が来訪し、一緒に読書をした。
『コッタ』を読み、書状を認めた。
砲艦「平遠」が鳩湾で浮流機雷によって沈没したと報じられた。300名の命が失われた。
奉天と遼陽の間で大きな戦闘が差し迫っていると報じられた。

10月13日木曜　天気　晴
日本の大勝利が報じられた。テムズ河岸に散歩した。
『コッタ』等を読んだ。夜オオタ氏が来訪した。

10月14日金曜　天気　晴
平田氏を訪問し、一緒に読書をした。
クロパトキンは退却中と報じられている。多くのロシアの大砲が接収された。
『コッタ』等を読んだ。

10月15日土曜　天気　晴
大きな戦闘が日本軍に有利にまだ続いている。かなりの数のロシア兵が捕虜となり、30以上の大砲が接収された。ステッセルの無線電報が日本軍によって傍受されていた。食料と弾薬が□□□。旅順の陥落が急速に近づいているようだ。スミス教授（キングスマウンド）を訪ねた。
紹介状をもらい、マンスフィールド・カレッジの学長先生に面会した。

Got a note of introduction to & saw the Principal of Mansfield College.

発信　A postal to Rev. Deacon
受信　An invitation from the Japanese minister.
　　　A letter from home.
　　　A postal from home.

日曜日の礼拝に通ったマンスフィールド・カレッジの現在のチャペル入口

10月16日日曜　天気　Fair

Attended the chapel service in Mansfield College. Mr. Hirata called, read *The Sketch Book* together. Mr. Ota called afterward, took tea together. Invited by Prof. Smith to dinner in the dining hall of Balliol College. Met several other professors. Came home 10 p.m.

Read *Cotta* &c.

10月17日月曜　天気　Foul　寒暖　London　59°2 p.m.

A great Japanese victory to Russian crushing defeat confirmed.
Went to Mr. Hirata's to read *The Sketch Book*.
Went to see Prof. Selincourt carrying a note of introduction from Prof. Smith & asked to attend his lecture on Shakespeare which he consented.
The Sha‒Ho battle still going on favorably to the Japanese. Had no

現在のマンスフィールド・カレッジのチャペルの内部

10月16日日曜　天気　晴
　マンスフィールド・カレッジのチャペルの礼拝に出席した。平田氏が来訪し『スケッチブック』を一緒に読んだ。後でオオタ氏が来訪し、お茶を共にした。スミス教授にベリオール・カレッジの食堂での夕食に招かれた。他の何人もの教授に会った。午後10時に帰宅した。
　『コッタ』等を読んだ。

10月17日月曜　天気　荒天　寒暖　ロンドン午後2時59°
　日本軍の大勝利とロシアの惨敗が確認された。
　平田氏のところに行って『スケッチブック』を読んだ。
　セリンコート教授のところに、スミス教授からの紹介状を持参し、彼のシェイクスピアの講義に出席させてくれるよう頼んで、許しをもらった。
　沙河海戦はいまも日本有利に進んでいる。暖炉に火を入れなかった。

fire.

10月18日火曜　天気　Foul　寒暖　London　66°2 p.m.

Attended Prof. Sweet's lecture on the Practical Study of Languages at the Taylor Institution.

Mr. Hirata called and read *The Sketch Book* together.

Called on Prof. Dyer, who had called in the morning when not in, and left notes of introduction to Profs. Raleigh & Sweet. He gave also a note of introduction to Mr. Whealer in Bodleian Library. Disagreeably warm. No fire.

受信　A postal from Mr. Kodama (Newcastle).

10月19日水曜　天気　Dull

Attended Prof. Raleigh's lecture on Chaucer at the "Schools." Bought a copy of Chaucer by Palland& another by Tuckwell, 1/- each.

The Sha-Ho battle still going on, some dozens guns under Gen. Yamada captured by the Russians on Saturday (16th). In other respects the Japanese are all victorious.

Went to Mr. Hirata's & read *The Sketch Book*.

発信　A letter to Mr. Fujie.
　　　A letter to Kodama.
受信　A postal from Mr. Shattack.

10月20日木曜

Attended Prof. de Selincourt's lecture on Shakespeare in the Examination Schools.

Bought a Copy of Prof. Dowden's *Shakespearian Primer* (1/-).

Mr. Hirata called & had usual reading.

10月18日火曜　天気　荒天　寒暖　ロンドン午後2時66°
　テイラー・インスティテューションで行われたスウィート教授の「言語の実際的研究」に関する講義に出席した。
　平田氏が来訪し、一緒に『スケッチブック』を読んだ。
　ダイアー教授を訪問した。彼は午前中留守中に来てくれて、ローリイ［注：Sir Walter Raleigh］教授とスウィート［注：Henry Sweet］教授への紹介状を置いて行ってくれていた。彼はまたボドリアン図書館のウィーラー氏への紹介状も書いてくれた。不快なほど暖かい。暖炉には火を焚いていない。

10月19日水曜　天気　曇天
　「スクールズ」でローリィ教授のチョーサーについての講義に出席した。ポラード［注：Alfred William Pollard］によるチョーサーの本を1冊、タックウェル［注：William Tuckwell］による別の本を買った（各1シリング）。
　沙河海戦はまだ続いている。山田［注：保永］少将の下の数十台の大砲が16日土曜日にロシア軍によって接収された。その他の点では日本軍が勝利している。
　平田氏のところに行き、『スケッチブック』を読んだ。

10月20日木曜
　セリンコート教授によるシェイクスピアの講義をエグザミネーション・スクールズ［注：大学内の試験に使われる大きな部屋］で受けた。
　ドーデン教授［注：Edward Dowden］の『シェイクスピア入門』を1冊購入した（1シリング）。

オックスフォード滞在日記　211

The Sha-Ho Battle reported to have been brought a lull.

発信　A postal to Mr. Shattack.

10月21日金曜　天気　Foul　寒暖　Warm

This is ninety ninth anniversary of Nelson and the Nelson's column in Trafalgar Square was decorated from top to foot. Much regret not to be in London.

Attended Prof. Raleigh's lecture on Chaucer.

Went to Mr. Hirata's to tea.

Disagreeably warm. Rained towards evening. Read a play &c.

発信　A letter to home.
　　　A letter to Mr. Hojo.
　　　Papers to Mr. Hojo.
　　　A postal to Mr. Ibaraki.
　　　A postal to Doi (U.S.).

10月22日土曜　天気　Fair

Read Chaucer & Shakespeare.

Took bath (public).

10月23日日曜　天気　Fair

Attended the chapel exercise of Mansfield College.

Went to Mr. Ota's for tea.

Read *the Sketch Book* with Mr. Hirata.

Read Shakespeare &c.

10月24日月曜　天気　Fair

Attended Prof. Selincourt's lecture.

平田氏が来訪し、いつもの読書をした。
沙河会戦は膠着状態にあると報じられた。

10月21日金曜　天気　荒天　寒暖　暖
今日はネルソンの99回目の記念日で、トラファルガー広場のネルソン記念塔は上から下まで飾り付けられている。ロンドンにいないのが大変残念だ。
ローリィ教授によるチョーサーの講義に出席した。
平田氏のところへお茶に行った。
不快なほど暖かい。夜になると雨が降った。戯曲等を読んだ。

10月22日土曜　天気　晴
チョーサーとシェイクスピアを読んだ。
入浴した（公衆浴場）。

10月23日日曜　天気　晴
マンスフィールド・カレッジのチャペルの礼拝に出席した。
オオタ氏のところにお茶に行った。
平田氏と『スケッチブック』を読んだ。
シェイクスピアその他を読んだ。

10月24日月曜　天気　晴
セリンコート教授の講義に出席した。

Read Shakespeare.

Went to the New Theater to see "Little Mary" in the evening.

English fishing boats (trawlers) were fired upon by Russian Baltic Fleet & two were killed (Friday night).

10月25日火曜　天気　Fair

Attended Dr. Sweet's lecture.

Read Chaucer & Shakespeare.

Went to Mr. Hirata's & read *the Sketch Book*. Took a walk to the church meadow.

Much comment was made on Baltic Fleet's outrage.

Mr. [　] called in the evening.

発信　Postal to Rev. Shattack, Miss Pope, Mrs. Walker, Chappell.
受信　Letters from home, Seki, Hashimoto & Midzuki.
　　　2 postcards from Kobayashi.
　　　Postcards from Shiomi, Miss Pope & Rev. Shattack.

10月26日水曜　天気　Foggy

Attended Prof. Raleigh's lecture.

Went to Mr. Yamazaki's for tea.

Mr. Ota called in the evening.

Read Chaucer &c.

10月27日木曜　天気　Foggy

Attended Prof. Selincourt's lecture.

Wrote letters for Japan.

Foggy & cold.

発信　A letter to Miss Snowdon.

シェイクスピアを読んだ。
夜はニュー・シアターに「リトル・メアリー」を観に行った。
英国の漁船（トロール船）がロシアのバルチック艦隊に発砲され、2名が死んだ（金曜夜）。

10月25日火曜　天気　晴
スウィート氏の講義に出席した。
チョーサーとシェイクスピアを読んだ。
平田氏のところに行って、『スケッチブック』を読んだ。チャーチ・メドウに散歩に行った。
バルチック艦隊の暴挙に多くの批判が沸き起こっている。
夜［氏名不明］氏が来訪した。

10月26日水曜　天気　霧
ローリィ教授の講義に出席した。
山崎氏のところにお茶を行った。
夜オオタ氏が来訪した。
チョーサー等を読んだ。

10月27日木曜　天気　霧
セリンコート教授の講義に出席した。
日本に送る書状を認めた。
霧が深く寒い。

　　　　Postals to home, Kobayashi, Yazima, Sekiguchi, and Nagano.

受信　A letter from home.

　　　A letter from Tanabe.

　　　A letter from Shiomi.

　　　A letter from Student (H. N. C.).

　　　A letter from Chappell.

　　　A letter from Sekiguchi (Manchester).

　　　Postcards from Yasui, Yoshimura, T. Hori, Kobinata, Matsui, Yajima, Mr. Walker, Nagano.

　　　A package of M.S. from Mr. Nagano.

10月28日金曜　天気　Fair　寒暖　57°

　　Attended Prof. Raleigh's lecture.

　　Left Oxford at 2:12 p.m. reached Paddington 3:30.

　　Went to see Mr. Suzuki at his lodging – Haverstock Hill, and went together to Tottenham court Rd. bought 2 dress shirts, gloves, collars, & ties (13s–10d). Dined at Mrs. Dale's.

発信　A postal to Mrs. Pope.
受信　A postal from Mrs. Pope.

10月29日土曜　天気　Fair

　　Went to the Yokohama Specie Bank, received £ 25-2-4.

　　Went to Chappell to try on dress suit & paid £ 6-6-0 for it.

　　Had lunch at Exeter Hall.

　　Bought 2 vols of Dr. Johnson's Shakespeare 1D each, Marion Crawford's *Paul Pataff* & *Dr. Claudin* 1/6 each, & works of Goldsmith 10d.

　　Visited Mrs. Maxwell.

10月28日金曜　天気　晴　寒暖　57°
ローリィ教授の講義に出席した。
オックスフォードを午後2時12分に発ち、パディントンに3時半に着いた。
鈴木氏に会いにハーバーストックヒルの下宿を訪ね、一緒にトッテナムコートロードに行って、礼服用の白シャツを2枚、手袋、カラーとネクタイ（13シリング10ペンス）を購入した。デイル夫人のところで食事をした。

10月29日土曜　天気　晴
横浜正金銀行に行き、25ポンド2シリング4ペンスを受け取った。
チャペルに礼服を試着に行って、6ポンド6シリング支払った。
エクセターホールで昼食を取った。
ジョンソン博士のシェイクスピアの本を2冊買い、1冊1ペニーだった。マリオン・クロフォードの『ポール・パトフ』と『ドクター・クローディン』をそれぞれ1シリング6ペンス、ゴールドスミスの作品を10ペンスで購入した。
マックスウェル夫人を訪問した。

10月30日日曜　天気　Misty

Attended the Ethical Meeting at the Hampstead Conservation in the morning. Went to tea at Mr. Deacon's in the afternoon.

10月31日月曜　天気　Misty

Went to the West End: bought cuff buttons & studs(£ 1-4-0).
Went to tea at Mr. Shattack's.

受信　A letter from Miss Snowdon.
　　　A parcel from Chappell.

11月

11月1日火曜　天気　Misty

Went to see Mr. Suzuki & went together to Gower st. bought some postcards. Took lunch at the West End. Visited the Postal Gallery. Took tea at the Lyan Piccadilly. Saw the model of St. Peter's Cathedral in Rome.

Baltic Fleet reported left vigo & British Fleet reported cleared for action.

受信　A postcard from Mr. Fukata.

11月2日水曜　天気　Fair

Went to the Sale for foreign missions at the Kensington Town Hall. There were tableaus of Japanese life. There are some mistakes. A lady dressed in a red underwear was one of the gross mistakes; a gentleman with Jinrikisha man's hat was another. But on the whole it was very good.

Went to see Mr. Nagano but was not in.

10月30日日曜　天気　霧

午前中ハムステッド・カンバセーションでの倫理集会に出席した。午後はディーコン氏宅にお茶に行った。

10月31日月曜　天気　霧　寒暖

ウェストエンドに行き、カフスボタンと飾りボタンを購入した（1ポンド4シリング）。
シャタック氏宅にお茶に行った。

11月

11月1日火曜　天気　霧

鈴木氏に会いに行って一緒にガワーストリートに行き何枚か葉書を購入した。ウェストエンドで昼食。郵便ギャラリーを訪問した。ライアンピカデリーでお茶を飲んだ。ローマのセント・ピーターズ大聖堂の模型を見た。
　バルチック艦隊はヴィゴを出発したと報じられ、英国艦隊は戦闘準備をしたと報じられた。

11月2日水曜　天気　晴

ケンジントンタウンホールで行われた外国伝道団のためのセールに行った。日本の生活を描いた絵があった。いくつか間違いがある。赤い下着を着た女性がひどい間違いの一つであり、人力車夫の帽子をかぶった紳士も同様であった。しかし全体的にはなかなかよかった。
　永野氏に会いに行ったが、不在であった。
　英国で最も有名なコメディアンのダン・レンズが亡くなった。（彼の収

Dan Lens, the most noted comedian of the day in England died. (His salary was ₤ 250 a week!).

発信　A letter & Sphere to home.
　　　A letter to Mr. Shi☐☐ & Mr. Midzuki.
　　　A postal to Y. Hori, Kobinata & Shi ☐☐.
　　　A letter to Yoshimura, Tanaka, Matsui.
受信　A letter from Mr. Flint.
　　　A letter from Mr. Hirata inclosing a letter from Mr. Nagaya.

11月3日木曜　天気　Fair
天長節

Went with Mr. Suzuki to Greenwich, visited the Naval College & saw the Royal Observatory from outside. Bought Living London II Vol 1 (8s)

Went to the Japanese Legation for the Celebration of the Emperor's birthday in the evening.

Came home half past 12.

発信　A letter to Mrs. Flint.
受信　A letter from Mr. Hirata.

11月4日金曜　天気　Fair
Visited National Portrait Gallery.

Went to dinner at Mrs. Flint's in the evening, met Mr. Wright (a statesman).

発信　A postal to Mr. Hirata.
　　　A package of book to home.
　　　2 postals to home.
受信　A package of books (Living London).

入は１週250ポンドであった！）

11月３日木曜　天気　晴
天長節
鈴木氏とグリニッジに行って、海軍大学を訪問し、王立天文台を外から見た。『リビング・ロンドンⅡ』第１巻を買った（８シリング）。
夜は天長節のお祝いに日本公使館に行った。
12時半帰宅。

11月４日金曜　天気　晴
ナショナル・ポートレイト・ギャラリーを訪ねた。
夜はフリント夫人宅に夕食に行き、ライト氏（政治家）に会った。

11月5日土曜　天気　Fair

London – Oxford

This is Guy Fawkes day, boys are seen dragging an effigy & begging for a small contribution to spend in a big bonfire which they have on the Heath.

Left Paddington at 1:45 p.m. reached Oxford at 3 p.m.

Bonfires were made in several places & cracking of fireworks were heard in different directions.

発信　Visiting Cards in an envelope to Mrs. Flint.

11月6日日曜　天気　Mist

Attended the service at the chapel of Mansfield College.

Mr. Hirata called & had tea together.

11月7日月曜　天気　Foul

Attended Prof. Selincourt's lecture on Shakespeare.

Went to Mr. Hirata's & read *The Sketch Book* (Board Head's Tavern) together.

Wrote letters in the evening.

発信　A letter to Mr. Nagano.
受信　A postal from Mr. Yoshimoto.

11月8日火曜　天気　Fair　寒暖　Cold

Attended Dr. Sweet's lecture on the Practical study of Languages.

Mr. Hirata called & read *The Sketch Book* together. Wrote letters.

11月5日土曜　天気　晴
ロンドン ―― オックスフォード。
　今日はガイ・フォークス・ディ［注：1605年の同日に、ガイフォークスとその一味が時の国王ジェームス1世殺害を企てた事件を記念して、ガイフォークスと呼ぶ人形を作り、1日中町中を引き回し、夜になって焼き捨てる風習がある］で、男子たちが人形を引き回し、ヒースの上で焚く大かがり火に使うための寄付を求める姿が見られた。
　パディントン駅を午後1時45分に出て、オックスフォードに午後3時に着いた。
　かがり火はいろんな場所で焚かれ、花火の音が四方八方から聞こえてきた。

11月6日日曜　天気　霧
マンスフィールド・カレッジのチャペルの礼拝に出席した。
平田氏が来訪し、茶を共にした。

11月7日月曜　天気　荒天
セリンコート教授によるシェイクスピアの講義に出席した。
平田氏のところへ行き、『スケッチブック』（居酒屋ボアーズヘッド）を一緒に読んだ。
書状を認めた。

11月8日火曜　天気　晴　寒暖　寒
スウィート博士の「言語の実際的研究」に関する講義に出席した。
平田氏が来訪し、一緒に『スケッチブック』を読んだ。書状を認めた。

オックスフォード滞在日記　223

発信　A postal to Mr. Yoshimoto.
受信　A letter from Sothern & Co.

11月9日水曜　天気　Windy　寒暖　Warm

Attended Prof. Raleigh's lecture.

Went to tea at Mr. Yoshimoto's.

Mr. Ota called in the evening.

The first November gale in the Channel reported.

Mr. Roosevelt elected U.S. President.

This is the birthday of King Edward VI. Some illuminations & decorations in London. In Oxford nothing special noticed.

発信　A letter to home.
　　　A postal to Mr. Fukata.
　　　A postal to Oshima.
　　　A letter to Mr. Nagaya.
　　　A package of newspapers to Mr. Hojo.
　　　A report to Monbusho.
　　　A package of a book (*Cotta Family*).

11月10日木曜　天気　Fair

Mr. Hirata & Mr. Ota called in the afternoon.

Spent the evening in reading.

Called on Mrs. Shaw in the afternoon.

受信　A letter from Miss A. C. Maitland.

11月11日金曜　天気　Fair

Attended Prof. Raleigh's lecture.

Went to Mr. Hirata's & read *The Sketch Book*.

11月9日水曜　天気　強風　寒暖　暖
ローリィ教授の講義に出席した。
好本氏［注：好本督(ただす)、後の近代盲人の福祉の先覚者］宅にお茶に行った。
オオタ氏が夜来訪した。
イギリス海峡で初めて11月の大風が報じられた。
ルーズベルト氏がアメリカ大統領に選ばれた。
　今日は国王エドワード6世の誕生日である。ロンドンはイルミネーションやデコレーションで彩られている。オックスフォードでは特別なことは何もなかったようだ。

11月10日木曜　天気　晴
午後平田氏とオオタ氏が来訪した。
夜は読書をして過ごした。
午後はショーン夫人を訪問した。

11月11日金曜　天気　晴
ローリィ博士の講義に出席した。
平田氏のところに行って『スケッチブック』を読んだ。

Mr. Ota called in the evening.

発信　A letter to home.
　　　A letter to Miss A. C. Maitland.
受信　A postal from Mr. Yamazaki.

11月12日土曜

Attended Prof. de Senlincourt's lecture.
Went to take a picture in group.
Mr. Hirata came to read together.
The surrender of Gen. Stassal reported by the telegram from Rome, but this public believe premature.

発信　Xmas cards & sailor-bay game to home.
受信　A letter & two postals from home.
　　　A postal from Mr. R. D. M. Shaw.

11月13日日曜　天気　Fair

Attended the service of Manchester College. Mansfield College Chapel was too full & no seat.
Went to Mr. Hirata's to read together.
Attended the evening service at Magdalene College.
The service is said to be the first in Oxford−New College the next−the second in Europe−St. Paul's the first.

11月14日月曜　天気　Fair

Attended Prof. de Selincourt's lecture.
Called on Mr. Yoshimoto to say a good bye.
Foggy towards the evening.

夜オオタ氏が来訪した。

11月12日土曜
セリンコート教授の講義に出席した。
グループ写真を取りに行った。
平田氏が来訪し、一緒に読書をした。
ステッセル将軍の降伏がローマからの電報で報じられたが、大衆はまだ時期尚早であると考えている。

11月13日日曜　天気　晴
マンチェスター・カレッジの礼拝に出席した。マンスフィールド・カレッジのチャペルは満員で席がなかった。
平田氏のところに行き、一緒に読書をした。
モードリン・カレッジの夜の礼拝に行った。
ここの礼拝はオックスフォードで最初に行われたものと言われている。（ニューカレッジが2番目）ヨーロッパでは2番目である。セント・ポール寺院が1番である。

11月14日月曜　天気　晴
セリンコート教授の講義に出席した。
別れの挨拶に好本氏を訪ねた。
夜になるにしたがって霧が出てきた。

Spent the afternoon in reading.

発信　A postal to Mr. Nagano.
　　　A postal toFlo.

11月15日火曜　天気　Fair
Attended Dr. Sweet's lecture.
Went to Mr. Hirata's to read together.
Took bath.
Very foggy in the morning, but cleared up to be a very fine day.

発信　A letter to Mr. Turbervill.
　　　A postal to Mr. Suzuki.
受信　A letter from Colonel Turbervill.
　　　A letter from Dr.Uchida (Heiderberg).
　　　A postal from Dr. Sasaki.
　　　Cheque from Chyuokinko.
　　　A postal from Monbusho.

11月16日水曜　天気　Foggy
Attended Prof. Raleigh's lecture.
Went to Mr. Hirata's to read together.
Attended Prof. Raleigh's public lecture.
Spent the whole evening in reading Japanese papers.

発信　A postal to Dr. Sasaki.
　　　A postal to Hr. Toda.

11月17日木曜　天気　Foggy
Spent whole day & evening in reading & writing.

午後は読書をした。

11月15日火曜　天気　晴
スウィート博士の講義に出席した。
平田氏のところへ行き、一緒に読書をした。
入浴した。
午前中は霧が深かったが、晴れて好天になった。

11月16日水曜　天気　霧
ローリィ教授の講義に出席した。
平田氏のところに一緒に読書をしに行った。
ローリィ教授の公開講義に出席した。
夜はずっと日本の新聞を読んで過ごした。

11月17日木曜　天気　霧
日中も夜もずっと読書と作文をして過ごした。

Mr. Hirata & Mr. Ota called in the afternoon.

発信　Dr. Ritter (Wien).
受信　A postcard from Col. Turbervill.
　　　A postal from Mr. Nagano.
　　　A postal fromFlo.
　　　A letter from Mr. Suzuki.

11月18日金曜　天気　Foggy

Attended Prof. Raleigh's lecture.

Col. Turbervill from Wales called. Mr. Hirata was here at the same time.

Mr. Ota called in the evening.

発信　A postal to Mr. Nagano.
　　　A postal to Suzuki.

11月19日土曜　天気　Wet

Attended Prof. de Selincourt's lecture in the morning.

Went to see Miss Maitland at Somervill College, & saw the library, dining halls &gymnasium.

Visited Mrs. [　] & arranged for the lesson on conversation.

11月20日日曜　天気　Fair

Attended Mansfield Chapel service.

Went to see Lady Markby (Sir William Markby) with Mr. Shaw & Mr. Hirata.

受信　A postcard from Herr Toda.

午後は平田氏とオオタ氏が来訪した。

11月18日金曜　天気　霧
ローリィ教授の講義に出席した。
ウェールズのターバヴィル大尉が来訪した。平田氏も同時にここにいた。
夜はオオタ氏が来訪した。

11月19日土曜　天気　じめじめした天気
午前中は、セリンコート教授の講義に出席した。
サマーヴィル・カレッジにメイトランド嬢に会いに行き、図書館、食堂、体育館を見学した。
　［氏名不明］夫人を訪ね、会話のレッスンをしてもらうことにした。

11月20日日曜　天気　晴
マンスフィールド・チャペルの礼拝に出席した。
　ショー氏と平田氏と共に、レディ・マクビー（サー・ウィリアム・マクビー）に会いに行った。

11月21日月曜　天気　Fair □□□　寒暖　40°

Attended Mr. de Selincourt's lecture.

Went to Mr. Hirata to read together.

Attended Prof. Raleigh's lecture on Richard Hukluyt's voyage in the schools.

Sleet towards the evening.

This was a Japanese mail day, but no letter from Japan.

Made an inquiry at the old lodging, but none had reached.

11月22日火曜　天気　Snowy　寒暖　36°

Attended Dr. Sweet's lecture.

Went to Miss Eva's to take a lesson on conversation.

Very cold, had snow accumulating about an inch deep.

受信　Registered letter enclosing a watch chain from Mr. Matsubara (Manchester).

11月23日水曜　天気　Fine　寒暖　36°
新嘗祭

Attended Prof. Raleigh's lecture.

Sent money order 12/3 to Mr. Matsubara.

No news from the theater of the war.

Weather fine, but very cold.

Went to Wadham College to see the Warden's Garden & the college garden with Mr. Shaw, Mrs. Andrew & Mr. Hirata.

Went to see the Chapel of Keble college.

Had snow in the evening.

11月21日月曜　天気　晴、□□□　寒暖　40°
セリンコート氏の講義に出席した。
平田氏宅をともに読書をするために訪問した。
スクールズでローリィ教授の「リチャード・ハルクートの航海」に関する講義に出席した。
夜になるにつれみぞれ模様になった。
今日は日本からの郵便が届く日であったが、日本から1通も来ていなかった。
前の下宿に問い合わせをしてみたが、1通も届いていなかった。

11月22日火曜　天気　雪　寒暖　36°
スウィート博士の講義に出席した。
エヴァ嬢のところへ行き会話のレッスンを受けた。
とても寒く、雪が1インチ程積もった。

11月23日水曜　天気　晴　寒暖　36°
新嘗祭
ローリィ教授の講義に出席した。
松原氏に12シリング3ペンスの為替を送付した。
戦場に関して何のニュースもない。
天候はよいが、とても寒い。
ワダム・カレッジに行って、ショー氏、アンドルー夫人、平田氏と共に「校長の庭園」と大学の庭園を見学した。
ケブル・カレッジのチャペルを見学に行った。
夜は雪が降った。

発信　A Registered letter enclosing 12/3 money order to Mr. Matsubara.
受信　A catalogue from Henry Sotheran & Co.

皇軍旅順砲台占領す。(37年)

11月24日木曜　天気　Fair　寒暖　27°
　No lecture today. Mr. Hirata called in the afternoon.
　Read *Ulysses* by Stephan Philips, very interesting.
　Attended the Union Dabate in the Club of Oxford Union Society in the evening. The questions for debate; "That this House approves Mr. Chamberlain's conception of Empire." The Hon. Sir J. A. Cockburn K. C. M. G., Ex-premier of South Australia took part.

受信　A postcard from Monbusho.

11月25日金曜　天気　Fair
　Attended Prof. Raleigh's lecture.
　Read *Ulysses*. Wrote letters.
　The weather fine, but very cold.
　Very little news of the war.
　Snowed during the night.

発信　4 packages of pictures to home.
　　　A letter to home.
　　　A package of books to Ibaraki & Tanabe.
　　　Receipt to Chyuokinko.
　　　A letter to Mr. Hojo.
　　　A letter to Mrs. Bosanquet.
受信　A postal from Mr. Matsubara.
　　　2 letters & 2 postals from home.

皇軍旅順砲台占領す。(37年)[注：旅順砲台の占拠は、杉森にとっても大きな出来事であり、日記の欄外の歴史上の出来事のところに記入している]

11月24日木曜　天気　晴　寒暖　27°
今日は講義がなかった。平田氏が午後来訪した。
スティーヴン・フィリップスの『ユリシーズ』を読んだ。大変面白い。
夜はオックスフォード・ユニオン・ソサエティというクラブのユニオン・ディベートに出席した。ディベートの問題は、「我々はチェンバレン氏の帝国についても概念を認める」であった。南オーストラリア前州知事であるコックバーン閣下が参加された。

11月25日金曜　天気　晴
ローリィ教授の講義に出席した。
「ユリシーズ」を読んだ。書状を認めた。
天候はよいが、大変寒い。
戦争のニュースはほとんどない。
夜の間に雪が降った。

11月26日土曜

Attended Prof. de Selincourt's lecture.

Went to take a lesson in conversation.

Attended Prof. [   ] lecture on Shakespeare in the afternoon in the schools.

Took bath. The weather fine, very cold.

No war news.

受信　A postal from Mr. Hirata.

11月27日日曜　天気　Foggy

Attended Mansfield Chapel service.

Mr. Bate, Hirata, Ota & Yamazaki came to tea.

11月28日月曜　天気　Fair

Attended Mr. de Selincourt's lecture. Mr. Hirata called & read together.

An assault & fierce fighting at Port Arthur reported.

The weather, a little milder.

発信　A letter to Mr. Hirayama (Clapham).
　　　A postal to Mr. Suzuki.

11月29日火曜　天気　Foul

Attended Dr. Sweet's lecture.

Went to take the lesson on conversation.

The weather much milder, streets are dirty by the thaw.

11月30日水曜　天気　Cloudy

Attended Prof. Raleigh's lecture.

Went to Mr. Hirata's to read together.

11月26日土曜
セリンコート教授の講義に出席した。
会話のレッスンを受けに行った。
午後はスクールズで［氏名不明］教授のシェイクスピアの講義に出席した。
入浴した。天候はよいが、とても寒い。
戦争のニュースはない。

11月27日日曜　天気　霧
マンスフィールド・チャペルの礼拝に出席した。
ベイト氏、平田氏、オオタ氏、山崎氏がお茶に来訪した。

11月28日月曜　天気　晴
セリンコート氏の講義に出席した。平田氏が来訪し共に読書をした。
旅順での一斉攻撃と熾烈な戦闘が報じられた。
天候は少し穏やかになった。

11月29日火曜　天気　荒天
スウィート博士の講義に出席した。
会話のレッスンを受けに行った。
天候はずいぶんと穏やかになったが、通りはぬかるみで汚い。

11月30日水曜　天気　曇
ローリィ教授の講義に出席した。
平田氏のところに共に読書をしに行った。

Went to see the play (Sweet Lavender) at the New Theatre. The play was written by Pinero.

受信　A postal from Mr. Hirayama.

12月

12月 1 日木曜　天気　Cloudy
Stayed at home in the morning. Went to take the lesson in the afternoon, & then went to the library (Bodleian).

This was the Queen of England's sixtieth birthday.

The weather is very mild.

12月 2 日金曜　天気　Cloudy
Attended Prof. Raleigh's lecture (the last in this term). The capture of the 203 meter Hill fort at Port Arthur was officially reported. This is the key to the northeastern fort & the capture of it is an important improvement towards the reduction of the stronghold.

The weather mild.

Mr. Hirata called & read together.

受信　A postal from Mr. Suzuki.

12月 3 日土曜　天気　Misty
Attended Mr. de Selincourt's lecture.

Bought works of Chaucer, English miscellaneous & c, at Blackwell, Broad St. (£ 5-7-6) possessed by late York Powell. Went to take a lesson.

ニュー・シアターに芝居を観に行った（スウィート・ラヴェンダー）。芝居はピネロ［注：当時人気の劇作家］の書いたものである。

12月

12月1日木曜　天気　曇
午前中は家にいた。午後はレッスンを受けに行き、それから図書館（ボドリアン）に行った。
今日は英国女王の60回目の誕生日である。
天候は大変穏やかである。

12月2日金曜　天気　曇
ローリィ教授の講義（今学期最後）に出席した。旅順の203高地要塞の占領が公式に報じられた。これは北東方向の要塞への重要拠点で、これを占領したことが要塞減少への重要な進展となっている。
天候は穏やかである。
平田氏が来訪し、一緒に読書をした。

12月3日土曜　天気　霧
セリンコート氏の講義に出席した。
ブロードストリートのブラックウェル書店でチョーサーの作品、英語関係をいろいろ、その他を購入した（5ポンド7シリング6ペンス）。これは故ヨーク・パウェル［注：英国の歴史家］が所有していたものだった。
レッスンを受けに行った。

12月4日日曜　天気　Misty

　Stayed all day at home. Mr. Hirata, Ota, Yamazaki called in the afternoon.

　The weather wet & rather warm.

　Read *Black Diamon*d.

発信　A postal to Flo.

12月5日月曜　天気　Fair

　Attended Mr. dee Selincourt's lecture in University College Hall.

　The weather very fine in the morning, showery in the afternoon.

　Took bath. Bought Hazlitt's Shakespeare (6/) & Facsimiles Quarto, Romeo and Juliet (5/6) . Both possessed by late York Powell.

受信　A postal from Mr. Kodama.

　　　A letter from Flory.

12月6日火曜　天気　Rain

　Attended Dr. Sweet's lecture--the last one.

　Went to take lesson in the afternoon.

　The weather very wet, but not cold.

　The sun rises today at 7:52 am. & sets 3:50 p.m.

12月7日水曜　天気　Fair

　Mr. Hirata called in the morning & dined.

　Called on Mr. Yamazaki in the afternoon expecting Profs. Motosa from London who failed to come.

　Prof. Motosa called in the evening.

　Wrote letters for Japan.

12月4日日曜　天気　霧
終日家にいた。午後平田氏、オオタ氏、山崎氏が来訪した。
天候は雨で、かなり暖かい。
『ブラック・ダイアモンド』を読んだ。

12月5日月曜　天気　晴
ユニバーシティ・カレッジ・ホールでのセリンコート氏の講義に出席した。
天候は午前中はよかったが、午後はにわか雨が降った。
入浴した。ハズリット［注：英国の作家、批評家］のシェイクスピア（6シリング）とロミオとジュリエットのファクシミリ・クアルト［注：四つ折り版の複写］、（5シリング6ペンス）。両方とも故ヨーク・パウエルが所有していたものだった。

12月6日火曜　天気　雨
スウィート博士の講義に出席した（最後の講義）。
午後はレッスンを受けに行った。
天候は悪いが、寒くはない。
今日は太陽は午前7時52分に昇り、午後3時50分に沈んだ。

12月7日水曜　天気　晴
平田が午前中に来訪し、食事をした。
午後は山崎氏を訪ね、ロンドンからモトサ教授が来るのを待っていたが、来なかった。
モトサ教授が夜来訪された。
日本への書状を認めた。

発信　A letter & Sphere to home.

　　　A letter to Tanabe, Ibaraki, Honma.

　　　A letter & calendars to Shinmi & Nagaya, Hori, Kurihara.

　　　Calendars to Miss Kiwaki, Miss Katagiri, Kobayashi, Shirani.

12月8日木曜　天気　Fair

Called on Mr. Hirata in the morning & went to the Wilberforce Hotel together to see Profs. Motosa & Fujioka who were not in. Called on & saw them in the afternoon visited Celdorian Theatre & Bodleian Library, St. Mary's Church & Indian Institution.

Went to see "The Comedy of Errors," Played by the Elizabethan stage society at the Town Hall. The play was all in the old costume.

The Russian fleets in the harbor of Port Arthur were all destroyed by the Japanese fire from 203 meter Hill.

発信　A postal to Mr. R. D. M. Shaw.

　　　A postal to Miss E. Pauling.

受信　A postal from Miss E. Pauling.

12月9日金曜　天気　Wet

Stayed at home & spent much of the time in Reading *Dr. Faustus* & *Black Diamond*.

Went to see Dr. Faustus played by the Elizabethan stage society at the Town Hall in the afternoon.

Mr. Ota called in the evening.

発信　A postal (to) Miss E. Pauling.

受信　A postal from Miss E. Pauling.

12月8日木曜　天気　晴

　午前中平田氏を訪問し、一緒にウィルバーフォースホテルにモトサ教授とフジオカ教授に会いにいったが、留守だった。午後訪問し二人に会い、セルドリアン劇場、ボドリアン図書館、セント・メアリーズ教会、インディアン学院を見学した。

　「間違いの喜劇」を観に行った。タウン・ホールでエリザベス朝舞台協会が演じた。芝居は全て古い衣装を着て行われた。

　旅順港のロシア艦隊は全て203高地からの日本軍の攻撃で破壊された。

12月9日金曜　天気　雨

　家にいて、ほとんどの時間を「ドクター・ファウスタス」と「ブラック・ダイアモンド」を読んで過ごした。

　午後はタウン・ホールでエリザベス朝舞台協会が演じる「ドクター・ファウスタス」を観に行った。

　夜はオオタ氏が来訪した。

12月10日土曜　天気　Wet

　Stayed at home reading in the forenoon.

　Went to take the lesson in the afternoon.

　Mr. Hirata called.

受信　2 postals & a letter from home.

12月11日日曜　天気　Fair Snow after

　Attended the service in Mansfield College.

　Met Mr. Hori from Cambridge. He called in the afternoon.

　Went to Mr. Norman Smith 12 Winchester Rd. to tea.

　The weather fair in the morning, in the afternoon grew colder & snowed.

12月12日月曜　天気　Fair

　Read *Black Diamond* & finished, rather interesting.

　Went to Mrs. Shaw's to tea.

　Mr. Ota called in the evening.

　Read *Dr. Faustus*.

受信　A letter from Mr. Nagaya.

12月13日火曜　天気　Fair

　Read *Dr. Faustus* and finished.

　Went to take the lesson.

　Took bath.

受信　A letter from Seki.

　　　Secondhand books Catalogue from Sotheran & Co.

12月10日土曜　天気　雨
午前中家にいて、読書をした。
午後はレッスンを受けに行った。
平田氏が来訪した。

12月11日日曜　天気　晴 後雪
マンスフィールド・カレッジの礼拝に出席した。
ケンブリッジから来たホリ氏に会った。彼は午後来訪した。
ウインチェスターロード12番のノーマン・スミス氏のところにお茶に行った。
午前中はよい天気であったが、午後はだんだん寒くなって雪が降った。

12月12日月曜　天気　晴
『ブラック・ダイアモンド』を読み、読了した。なかなかおもしろかった。
ショー夫人宅にお茶に行った。
夜オオタ氏が訪ねてきた。
『ドクター・ファウスタス』を読んだ。

12月13日火曜　天気　晴
『ドクター・ファウスタス』を読んで、読了した。
レッスンを受けに行った。
入浴した。

12月14日水曜　天気　Fair

Went to Mrs. Pauling to tea.

Spent most of the day in Reading.

12月15日木曜　天気　Fair

Went to take the lesson.

Went to the Smiths (Norman) to tea.

Went to the Glee-men concert at the Town Hall.

発信　A letter to home.

　　　A letter to Seki.

　　　A letter to Mr. Obana.

12月16日金曜　天気　Fair

Spent most of the day in reading.

Mr. Ota called.

The weather was disagreeably warm.

発信　A postal to home.
受信　A letter from Mr. Miyachi.

　　　A letter & postal from home.

12月17日土曜　天気　Fair　寒暖　56°

Went to take the lesson. (pd. 12/- for 12 lessons.)

Called on Mr. A. L. Smith to say a good bye.

Called on Mr. Hirata.

The weather warm.

受信　A copy of Catalogue from H. N. C.

12月14日水曜　天気　晴
ポーリング夫人のところにお茶に行った。
ほとんどの時間を読書をして過ごした。

12月15日木曜　天気　晴
レッスンを受けに行った。
スミス家（ノーマン）にお茶に行った。
タウンホールで行われたグリーメンコンサートに行った。

12月16日金曜　天気　晴
1日の大半を読書して過ごした。
オオタ氏が来訪した。
不快なほど暖かい。

12月17日土曜　天気　晴　寒暖　56°
レッスンを受けに行った。（12回のレッスンに12シリング支払った。）
別れの挨拶をしにA.L.スミス氏を訪ねた。
平田氏を訪ねた。
暖かい。

12月18日日曜　天気　Fair

　Attended St. Mary Virgin Church in the morning, Magdalene College Chapel service in the evening.

　The weather very mild.

12月19日月曜　天気　Foggy

　Called on Prof. Raleigh, Mr. Dyer, Mr. de Selincourt, the Shaws & the Paulings for leaves taking.

　The weather cold & very foggy all the day.

　Took bath.

発信　A letter to Mr. A. R. Smith.
　　　Postals to Dr. Uchida & to the student of H. N. C.
　　　The view book of Cardiff to home.

12月20日火曜　天気　Fair

　Left Oxford for Stratford-on-Avon at 11:55 am.& reached Stratford 2 p.m. Changing the train at Leamington—took a walk to the park while waiting.

　Lodged at Mrs. Coak's I Old Town Stratford-on-Avon.

　Stratford is at the distance of 82ms from London.

発信　A postal to Tomiyasu.
　　　A postal to Kiuchi.
　　　A postal to Flo.

12月21日水曜　天気　Foggy

　Left Stratford for Charlecote (5ms), saw the Charlecote House (outside), the Tumble-down stile, & the church.

　Went to Hampton Lucy village, stopped at an inn & had a pint of ale;

248

12月18日日曜　天気　晴
午前中はセント・メアリー・ヴァージン教会に出席した。夜はモードリン・カレッジのチャペルの礼拝に出席した。
天候は穏やかである。

12月19日月曜　天気　霧
ローリィ教授、ダイア氏、セリンコート氏、ショー家、ポーリング家を訪れ、別れの挨拶をした。
天候は終日寒く、霧が深かった。
入浴した。

12月20日火曜　天気　晴
午前11時55分、オックフフォードをストラットフォード・オン・エイボンに向けて発ち、ストラットフォードに午後2時に着いた。レミントンで列車を乗り換え、待ち時間の間公園まで散歩した。
ストラットフォード・オン・エイボンのオールドタウン1番コーク夫人宅に宿を取った。
ストラットフォードはロンドンから82マイルの距離である。

12月21日水曜　天気　霧
ストラットフォードを発ってチャールコート（5マイル）へ向い、チャールコート・ハウス（外）、タンブル・ダウン・スタイル［注：柵を押し下げる踏み越し段］と教会を見学した。

オックスフォード滞在日記　249

posted postcards to Japan.

　　　Taking Warwick road, returned to Stratford at 3 p.m.

　　　The weather foggy & very cold.

　　　Reported very thick fog in London.

発信　A postal to home.
　　　A postal to Mr. Hojo from Hampton Lucy.
受信　A postal from Mr. Wachi.

12月22日木曜　天気　Foggy

　　Went to Birmingham by 11:45 train (22ms) & visited the Picture Gallery & Museum, the Free Library & bought a copy of the catalogue of the Shakespeare Memorial Library (a part of the Free Library).

　　The weather was very foggy − so thick that an could hardly see six feet ahead. Returned to Stratford 7:30 p.m.

発信　A postal to home (from Birmingham).
　　　A postal to Mr. Ota.
受信　A postal from Mr. Ota.
　　　A postal from Mr. Wachi.

12月23日金曜　天気　Foggy

　　Bought a copy of *Stratford Guide Book,* a copy of *Stratford-upon-Avon*

ハンプトン・ルーシー村に行って、宿屋に立ち寄って、エールを1パイント飲んで、日本への葉書を投函した。
　ウォリック・ロードを通って、ストラットフォードに午後3時に帰った。
　天候は霧が深く、とても寒い。
　ロンドンでは大変霧が深いと報じられた。

「チャールコート」（Sidney Lee 著 *Stratford-on-Avon* から Edward Hull によるイラスト）

12月22日木曜　天気　霧

　11時45分の列車でバーミンガム（22マイル）に行き、写真ギャラリーと博物館、フリー図書館を訪問し、シェイクスピア・メモリアル・ライブラリー（フリー図書館の一部）の目録を1冊購入した。
　天候は、霧が深く、6フィート先も見えないくらいだった。午後7時半にストラットフォードに帰った。

12月23日金曜　天気　霧

　『ストラットフォード・ガイドブック』を1冊と、『スケッチブック』の

from The Sketch Book. (2/6).

The weather foggy & cold.

発信　Xmas greetings to Flo.
　　　Xmas greetings to Miss Eva Pauling.
受信　Xmas greetings from Maxie.

12月24日土曜　天気　Less foggy

Visited Shakespeare's Memorial Building & the Birthplace.

The weather less foggy, but very cold, trees were covered with the hoarfrost.

受信　Xmas greetings from Miss Lily Walkers.
　　　Xmas greetings from Mr. Kodama.
　　　A postal from Mr. Yamazaki.

12月25日日曜　天気　Cloudy

Attended the service in the Holy Trinity Church in the morning.

Took a walk to the Old Mill & further into the country & then to Shottery —Anne Hathaway Cottage.

Dined with the family. The weather milder, not foggy.

発信　A postal to Miyachi.
　　　A postal to Mr. Kodama.
受信　Xmas greetings from Mr. Shaw.
　　　A postal from Miss Eva Pauling.

12月26日月曜　天気　Fair

Visited the Memorial Theatre & went over the green rooms, visited the Old Lucy mill, the Birhplace, the Red Horse Hotel, had tea & saw

中の「ストラットフォード・アポン・エイボン」を1冊購入した（2シリング6ペンス）。
　天候は霧が出て寒い。

12月24日土曜　天気　薄霧
シェイクスピアの記念堂と生家を訪問した。
霧は少しは薄れたが、とても寒く、木々は霜で真っ白になっている。

12月25日日曜　天気　曇
午前中はホーリー・トリニティ・チャーチの礼拝に出席した。
　オールドミルへ、そしてさらに田舎へ、そしてショッタリーの「アンハサウェイの家」へと散歩した。
　家族と食事を共にした。天候は穏やかに、霧も晴れた。

12月26日月曜　天気　晴
　メモリアル・シアターを訪問し、グリーンルーム［注：楽屋］を見て回り、オールド・ルーシー・ミルと生家、レッドホースホテル［注：『スケッ

Irving's room, chairs, & scepter (poker).

発信　A postal to Mr, Togawa, Mr. Shimazaki, Mr. Suzuki.
受信　2 letters & a postal from home.
　　　A letter from Monbusho.
　　　A letter from Akidzuki.

「レッドホースホテル」（Sidney Lee 著 *Stratford-on-Avon* から Edward Hull によるイラスト）

12月27日火曜　天気　Cloudy

Stratford-on-Avon − Warwich − Leamington

　Left Stratford at 2:30 pm., reached Warwick 3 p.m., then by the train reached Leamington at 4:30 p.m. Took lodging at 9, Dover Place.

　Took bath at the Royal Pump Room.

　Saw the play "She stoops to conquer" at the Theatre Royal.

発信　A letter & a postal to home.
　　　A postal to Akidzuki.
　　　A postal to Mr. Wachi.
　　　A postal toNakanome.
　　　A postal toTanaka &c.

チブック』を書いたワシントン・アーヴィングが宿泊していた部屋がある］を訪ね、お茶を頂き、アーヴィングの部屋とイスと王笏（火かき棒）［注：王の持つ笏をかたどった火かき棒］を見た。

現在のレミントン・スパのロイヤル・パンプ・ルーム

12月27日火曜　天気　曇
ストラットフォード・オン・エイボン ── ウォリック ── レミントン
　ストラットフォードを午後2時半に発ち、ウォリックに午後3時に着き、それから列車で午後4時半にレミントンに着いた。宿をドーバープレイス9番に取った。
　ロイヤル・パンプ・ルームで入浴した。
　ロイヤル劇場で「シー・ストゥープス・トゥ・コンカー」という芝居を観た。

Postals to Mrs. B □□□.

New year greetings to Miss Lily Walker.

受信　Xmas greetings from Mrs. Shaw.

12月28日水曜　天気　Cloudy

Visited Kenilworth Castle (5ms). Came back by the way of Warwick, walking all the going & back. The road & the surrounding scenery is beautiful.

The weather mild, road bad by the thaw.

Went to see the play, "School of Scandal," at the Theatre Royal.

The sun rises at 8:07 am, sets at 3:56 p.m.

発信　2 postals to home (From Kenilworth).

A postal to Mr. Hojo (From Kenilworth).

受信　A postal from Herr Toda.

12月29日木曜

Visited Warwick Castle & saw the garden & inside of the Castle. Went up the tower of St. Mary's Church.

Walked all the way going & back (2ms from Leamington). The walk along the river Leam is very beautiful.

発信　2 postals to home (from Warwick).

受信　Postals from Mr.Suzuki (from Paris) & from Mr. Ota.

12月30日金曜　天気　Fair

Lemington – Oxford

Went about sight-seeing in Leamington in the morning. Left Leamington for Oxford at 3:15 p.m. & reached Oxford 4:09.

Lodged at 46, Southmoor Rd. The weather fair, but very windy.

12月28日水曜　天気　曇

ケニルワース城（5マイル）を訪ねた。ウォリック経由で帰った来た。行きも帰りもずっと歩いた。通りや周囲の景色が美しい。

天候は穏やかで、道はぬかるんで悪い。

「スクール・オブ・スキャンダル」という芝居を観にロイヤル劇場に行った。

太陽は午前8時7分に昇り、3時56分に沈んだ。

12月29日木曜

ウォリック城を訪ね、城の庭園や内部を見学した。セントメアリー教会の塔を登った。

行きも帰りもずっと歩いた（レミントンから2マイル）。リーム川沿いの歩道はとても美しい。

12月30日金曜　天気　晴

レミントン ── オックスフォード

午前中はレミントンを観光して回った。午後3時15分にレミントンを発ってオックスフォードに向い、4時9分にオックスフォードに着いた。

サウスムアロード46番に宿泊した。天候はよいが、風がとても強い。

Found letters & postals from Japan waiting.

受信　A letter & postal from home.
　　　A postal from Monbusho.
　　　Postals from Messrs. Mon☐☐ & Ibaraki.
　　　A letter from Mr. C. Bone (from Warwick).
　　　A letter from Flo.

12月31日土曜　天気　Fair

Oxford − London

Went to see Mr. Hirata at Rose Lane, settled account.

Left Oxford for London at 2:20 p.m. Took lodging at 44, Stanley Gardens Hampstead London (reaching there 4 p.m.). The weather very fine & mild.

A great progress reported at Port Arthur on the push of the besieger more forts being taken. Sat up to watch the year at midnight sang songs, exchanged greetings.

Ehr-lung-shan captured.

受信　The student.

日本からの書状と葉書が待っていた。

12月31日土曜　天気　晴
オックスフォード――ロンドン
　ローズレインに平田氏を訪ね、清算をすませた。
　2時20分にオックスフォードを発ち、ロンドンに向かった。ロンドンのハムステッドのスタンリー・ガーデンズ44番に宿泊した（そこに午後4時についた）。天候はとてもよく、穏やかである。
　旅順での大きな進展が報じられ、包囲軍の攻撃により、日本軍がより多くの要塞を占領している。寝ずに起きていて、12時に年が明けるのを見て、歌を歌い、新年のあいさつを交わした。
　日本軍が二龍山を占拠した。

現在のプリムローズヒル

住所人名録について

　巻末についている「住所人名録」は、「住所」「電話」「氏名」「郷国」の欄があり、留学生仲間や親交があった現地の人々の名前と住所が記されている。同一人物が複数回記載されている場合もある。

　「電話」「郷国」の欄には記載がないので、この2つの欄を削除し、編者が諸資料及び日記の内容から推察される人物情報を記載した。当時の杉森が持っていた友人関係をうかがい知ることができると同時に、ここに記された人々についてもその存在の重要な証拠となると思われる。

住所	名前	編者注
Ausbacher str. 17 IR, Berlin	K. Toda	戸田海市。京都帝国大学法科大学助教授。文部省留学生。ベルリンに留学しているためか、日記中にはMr. ではなくHerrという敬称がつけられている。
XIX Wien, Billat str. 19. OsterreichWigarum	A. Nakanome	中目覚。広島高等師範学校教授。文部省留学生。
22, Walton Crescent, Oxford	K. Hirata	平田喜一（禿木）。東京高等師範学校教授。文部省留学生。
5, Stanley Villas, Amershaw Buck	Miss C. L. Burnside	2月に一度手紙を出している。
S, Vedast 25 Calton Rows, Putney, S. W.	Miss M. Snowdon	杉森をお茶に招いている。11月1日に日本に行く予定が記されている。
312, Camden Road, W.	Dr. W. N. Whitney	2月に日本人キリスト教徒の集まりで会っている。Dr. Hortonへの紹介状を書いてくれた。
82, Gower str. London	S. Doi	土井助三郎。文部省留学生。帰国後名古屋高等工業学校初代校長。
	A. Kumamoto	隈本有尚。東京高等商業学校教授。文部省留学生。福岡県立尋常中学修猷館館長時代に杉森も在職していた。
72, Glocester str. New Castle on Tyne	R. Kodama	8月、ニューカッスルオンタインを訪れた際お世話になった。

住所	名前	編者注
83, Park Rd., New Castle on Tyne	S. Kato	ニューカッスルオンタイン在住で，3月に手紙をやりとりしている。8月に当地を訪ねた時には案内してくれた。
195, Plymouth Grove Manchester	S. Kobayashi	マンチェスターを訪問した際にお世話になった。
	Omiya, K.	ニューカッスルオンタインを一緒に見学した。
13, Oak Hall Rd. Newstead	Mr. H. L. Burnside	英語の個人レッスンを受けていた。
Christ Church Vicarage 10, Cannon Place, Hampstead, N. W.	Rev. A. E. Deacon	教会の牧師。お茶に招かれている。
10, Randolph Rd. Maida Hill. W.	Miss A. Weber	英語の個人レッスンを受けていた。
19, Bradiston Rd, St. Peter's Park W.	Mr. J. Lloyd	教えている学校を見学に行っている。親しく付き合っていた。
"Bankside," Brondesbury Park, N. W.	Mr. T. Kachi	加地利夫。三井物産社員。
40, St. Mary's Mansion, St. Mary's Terrace, Paddington W. (Near Bishop Rd. Station)	Mr. A. Ishii	郵船会社社員。杉森がロンドンに着いたとき迎えに来た。
3, Adden Brook Place, Cambridge	Mr. TK. Hori	12月にケンブリッジからオックスフォードを訪ねた。
Abenetry House, Mount Vernon, Henry street N. W.	Rev. Percy Shattack	牧師。家に招かれるなど親しくしている。
3, Halford Hampstead N. W.	Mrs. M. B. Bartrum	4月に家族と一緒に教会に行っている。6月に家を訪問している。
5, Mornington Avenue West Kensington., W.	Dr. G. Uchida	内田銀蔵。明治38年から広島高等師範学校教授。文部省留学生。
90, Brondesbury Rd. Kilburn	Mr. S. Mimoto	三本。郵船会社の社員。
23, Heath Hurst Rd. Hampstead	Mr. Taylor	5月にお茶に招いてくれた。
764, Coleherne Court S. Radcliffe Gdns. Kensington S. W.	Capt. Lacock	6月に日本人会で会い，その後，家を何度も訪問するなど親しくしていた。

住所	名前	編者注
17, Sinclair Gardens Kensington, W.	Mr. B. Nagano	永野武一郎。広島高等師範学校教授。文部省留学生。
Bradfield College, Reading	Mr. F. M. Ingram	7月にブラッドフィールド・カレッジを見学した時に案内してくれた。
33, Leinster Ave. East Sheer Mortlake	J.E. Melhuish	6月終わりから7月始めにかけて手紙のやり取りをしている。
7, Charlotte Str. Fitzray Square	Dr. J. Ritter	ドクトル・ヤコブ・リットル。ロンドンで同宿だったオーストリア人。
Wien I Universitat, Englisches Seminar	〃	ドクトル・リットルのウィーンの住所。
Wien II ObereDonaustraze, 13, I Stock F	〃	ドクトル・リットルのウィーンの住所。
Parmiter's School Approach Rd. Cambridge Heath	S. W. Daddo	7月に見学に行ったパルミターズスクールの教頭先生。
12, Eton Ave, Hampstead. N. W	Mr. W. Y. Maxwell	親しくつきあい、度々お茶や食事に招いてくれる。
c/o A. R. Brown Mac Farlane &Co. 34, West George St. Glasgow.	C. Isono. 磯野長蔵（明治屋）	9月にグラスゴーを訪問した際お世話になった。当時明治屋副社長。
90, Brondesbury Rd. Kilburn	Mrs. Rowlan (Caretaker)	三本氏の大家。
7, Broadhurst-Gdns, Finchely Road.	Mrs. Giles (Boarding house)	下宿屋の大家。Maxwell 夫人の紹介で部屋を見に行った。
Fenchurch St. E. C.	Worrall & Robey (Stationer)	
6, Upper Bakest. (Girl's high school)	Miss Strong	5月に訪問したチャーチ・オブ・イングランド女子高校の教頭。
6, York Place, Baker st. (Bedford Col. for Women)	Mrs. Hurlbatt	6月に訪問したベッドフォード女子大学の校長。
Graham st. Eton Sqr. (Girl's high shool)	Miss Lewis	6月に訪問したチャーチ・オブ・イングランド女子高校の校長。

住所	名前	編者注
19, Provast Rd. N. W.	Mr. G. Walter C. Maile	
Widbury, Ware.	Rev. Barclay Buxton	8月に Widbury, Ware に招待してくれた。
90, Brondesbury Rd. Kilburn	Mrs. Rowlan (三本君宅)	郵船会社の社員三本宅の大家。
52, Weltje Rd. Hammersmith	Mrs. Cape (永野君下宿)	文部省留学生永野武一郎の下宿の大家。
Rose Lane Flower Nursery, High St. Oxford	Mr. K. Hirata	平田喜一（禿木）の下宿。
26, Richmond Rd. Oxford	Miss Blake	
105 East 54th St. N. Y.	S. Taniguchi	
15, Chalfont Rd. Oxford	Mrs. Shaw	お茶に招かれたり，一緒に出かけるなど親交が深かった。
143, Fordwych Rd. Brondesbury N. W.	Mr. Watanabe	Widbury, Ware に一緒に行った。
15, Chalfont Rd. Oxford	Mr. R. D. M. Shaw (Wadham)	オックスフォード大学ワダム・カレッジの教員で，家族ぐるみで親しくしていた。
The King's Mound, Mansfield Rd. Oxford	Mr. A. L. Smith (Balliol)	オックスフォード大学ベリオール・カレッジの教員で，セリンコートの講義を受講する紹介状を書いてくれた。カレッジの食堂でのディナーにも招いてくれた。
bei Freu Muller Landfriedstr. 7 Heidelberg, Germany	Dr. G. Uchida	内田銀蔵のドイツ・ハイデルベルクの住所。
Yokohama Specie Bank Albert Building, Horuby Row, Fort, Bombay	Mr. Y. Hara	横浜正金銀行の行員で，一緒に英作文の練習をしていた。
Sunbury Lodge Oxford	Mr. Louis Dyer (Balliol)	オックスフォード大学ベリオール・カレッジの教員で、ローリィやスウィートの講義を受講する紹介状を書いてくれた。
12. Winchester Rd. Oxford	Mr. Norman Smith (Mansfield)	オックスフォード大学マンスフィールド・カレッジの教員で、12月上旬に何度かお茶に招いてくれた。

住所	名前	編者注
46. Southmoor Rd. Oxford	Mr. F. Bate (Balliol)	オックスフォード大学ベリオール・カレッジの教員で，11月27日平田らとお茶に来た。
8. Kensington Rd. Oxford	Miss E. Pauling	12月上旬お茶に招いてくれた。
Burn Side, Cole Park, Twickenham Lawn	Mr. Hirata	平田喜一（禿木）の下宿。

解　説

安部規子

杉森此馬について

　杉森家は福岡県柳川市の教育に深く関わってきた家である。旧柳川藩士の家系で，父憲正は旧藩では要職を務め，廃藩置県後も柳川師範学校付属中学校長始め重要な役職を歴任した。此馬の妹シカは明治28（1895）年に私塾「杉森女紅会」を創立し，大正期には女学校へ，戦後は高等学校（現在の杉森高等学校）へと発展させ，柳川の女子教育に尽くした人物であった。

　杉森此馬については，杉森研究の第一人者であった広島大学名誉教授の故松村幹男氏は，「広島高等師範英語教授・杉森此馬」の中で，「杉森は同校（注：広島高等師範学校を指す）最初の英語教授であり，英語科主任であり，英語教員養成の骨格を作り上げた人であり，またいちはやく phonetic symbols を学生に教えた人であり，雑誌『英語教授』編集の一角を担い，英語教育研究への道を開くという意義ある仕事を残した人」と評している。

　田邉祐司氏は，「日本英語音声教育史：杉森此馬の指導観」を始めとする論文において杉森の英語音声教育の面に焦点を当てて研究している。

　次ページの表は両氏の論文に示された杉森の略歴に基づいて作成したものである。安政5（1858）年，現在の福岡県柳川市で生まれた杉森は，熊本洋学校でL.L.ジェーンズに英語を学んだ後，郷里の福岡県立柳川師範学校を卒業し，さらに東京築地一致英和学校に学んだ。卒業後は明治学院で教員を務め，明治23（1890）年には同校教授となった。明治27（1894）年に文部省英語教員検定試験に合格し，福岡県の尋常中学修猷館及び茨城

県尋常中学の教諭を務めた。その後山口高等学校教授時代に校長北条時敬とのつながりができ，校長となる北条に請われて第四高等学校，さらには明治35（1902）年に新設された広島高等師範学校に教授として赴任することになった。2年間の英米への留学を終えて明治39（1906）年に帰朝した後は，広島高等師範学校英語科主任を命じられ，学生への英語音声教育を

杉森此馬の略歴

年代	事項
安政5（1858）年3月25日	現在の福岡県柳川市に生まれる。
明治7（1874）年	熊本洋学校に入学。ジェーンズから英語を習う。
明治9（1876）年	福岡縣々立柳河師範学校入学
明治13（1880）年	東京築地一致英和学校（後の明治学院）に入学
明治17（1884）年	同校卒業
明治18（1885）年	明治学院助教授
明治23（1890）年	明治学院教授
明治27（1894）年7月	文部省英語教員検定試験合格
明治27（1894）年7月	尋常中学修猷館雇教員
明治27（1894）年10月	尋常中学修猷館教諭
明治27（1894）年11月	茨城県尋常中学教諭
明治30（1897）年	山口高等学校教授
明治31（1898）年	第四高等学校教授
明治35（1902）年	広島高等師範学校教授
明治36（1903）年12月	2年間英米に留学
明治39（1906）年2月	帰朝
明治39（1906）年5月	師範学校中学校高等女学校教員等夏期講習会講師
明治39（1906）年12月	The English Teachers' Magazine（教文館）創刊　編集顧問
明治40（1907）年5月	師範学校中学校高等女学校教員等夏期講習会講師
明治42（1909）年9月	師範学校中学校高等女学校教員等夏期講習会講師
明治43（1910）年	休職して旅順工科学堂教務嘱託
明治44（1911）年4月	広島高等師範学校復職
大正2（1913）年	旅順工科学堂教授
大正12（1923）年6月	旅順工科大学予科教授
大正14（1925）年	帰国
昭和7（1932）年	成城女学校（昭和10年まで）
昭和11（1936）年	永眠

担当するばかりでなく，同年に始まった「師範学校中学校高等女学校教員等夏期講習会」の講師を同年，翌明治40（1907），明治42（1909）年，明治45（1912）年と務め，英米留学の成果を大いに発揮している。

また『英語教授』（*The English Teachers' Magazine*）を創刊し，英語発音に関する論文を発表した。

杉森此馬の広島高等師範学校教授の辞令
（柳川古文書館蔵）

その後明治43（1910）年に杉森は旅順に移っている。関東都督府民政長官となった従兄弟である白仁武に招聘され旅順工科学堂に勤めるために広島高師を休職，その後大正2（1913）年に辞職し，旅順工科学堂の教授になった。

それ以降，杉森は『英語教授』（*The English Teachers' Magazine*）の編集からも手を引き，日本の英語教育界からは姿を消していったようだ。

従って，英語教育に関して杉森が最も活動的で，顕著な貢献をしたのは明治36（1903）年の留学から明治42（1909）年までの広島高師教授であった時期と言える。

最後に，家族について述べると，杉森は妻ウメとの間に一男四女をもうけている。この日記を柳川古文書館に寄贈された髙月三世子氏のお母様が三女北村孝氏で，孝氏は東京女子大学名誉教授で英語学を専門とされた。また日記を含む「杉森此馬関連資料」を長年保管してきたのは杉森の帰朝後に生まれた四女のエイ氏で，エイは「英国」の「英」の字が当てられているとのことである。

1900年頃の文部省外国留学生

辻直人著『近代日本海外留学の目的変容—文部省留学生の派遣実態について—』によると，杉森が留学した1900年代は，文部省の海外留学生派遣制度の目的が変容した時期とされている。

この制度の主要な目的は、まず1880年代から1890年代においては、東京帝国大学の教員を補充することであり、留学生は東京大学卒業生の中から選ばれていた。その後、1900年から広島高師を含め十数校の官立高等教育機関が設立され、その教育体制の充実が目的となった。また、留学生の人選には批判も多く、

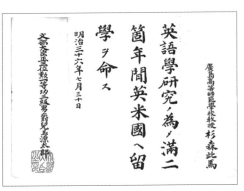

杉森此馬の2年間の留学辞令（柳川古文書館蔵）

留学が学問研究のためではなく、遊興か単なる留学生自身の昇進のためのものになっている、との批判があり、文部省は留学生の研究の管理を強めるようになった。そのような中で杉森此馬は「英語学研究」を目的として英国・米国へ2年間の留学を命じられた。

同時期の留学生として、夏目金之助（漱石）の他に東京高等師範学校教授岡倉由三郎がいる。岡倉はロンドン、パリ、ベルリンで英文学、語学教授法、音声学を学び、帰国後著作にその成果をまとめた。

平田諭治氏が「岡倉由三郎ロンドン大学講演考―背景と経緯」を始めとする論文で明らかにしているように、留学によって、研究者として飛躍を遂げたばかりでなく、日露戦争中とその後における世界情勢の中で日本の立場を説明するという大役も果たした。一方で明治36（1903）年に帰朝した夏目の留学は文部省が満足する成果をあげず、杉森は出発前に以下の注意を受けたとしている（「英語教育批判会―中等学校英語教育の諸問題―」）。

　私が洋行を命ぜられました時に文部省に招ばれて注意を受けたことがあります。私の前に夏目君が行つたのですが、文部省の人が申しますには夏目君のように下宿に引籠つて本ばかり読んで居て貰つては困る。もっと外国人の生活、実際の生活を見て来てほしいと注文です。

留学時の杉森の年齢は40代半ばで、留学生の中でかなり年長である。前掲の『近代日本海外留学の目的変容—文部省留学生の派遣実態について—』の巻末資料「文部省留学生一覧表」を見ると、当時の留学生のほとんどは20～30歳代で40歳代は非常に少ない。しかしながら、杉森の留学生活は多くの人々との関わりにより豊かなものになっている。同じ下宿の外国人や視察先の教育機関や日曜日の教会で出会う人々と積極的に交流すると共に、日本人の中では、専攻が異なる文部省留学生や現地企業の日本人とも親交を深め、小旅行中には産業革命の中心的役割を果たしたマンチェスターやニューカッスルオンタインで最新の科学技術を目の当たりにし、グラスゴーでは日本の戦艦が建造される造船所を見学している。日露戦争中であり、杉森もまた国際社会における日本の状況を強く意識していた。

留学生活の実際と成果

当時の留学生活とはどのようなものであったのか、日記の内容から考えてみたい。

最初の日本語の部分は、国のために留学しようとする決意と使命感にあふれ、その気持ちを詠んだ歌も多く作られている。また航路についてもよく研究しており、地理的、歴史的知識の豊富さは驚くほどである。

杉森は明治学院では、英語に加えて「地理」「植物」の授業も担当し、明治26 (1893) 年に『政治天然万国地理提要（丸善株式会社書店）』という世界の地理に関する重要な情報をまとめた本を出している。友人として立花小一郎（同郷の軍人・後の福岡市長）と徳富蘇峰（熊本洋学校の同窓生・評論家）が巻頭に言葉を寄せている。緒言によると、地理の勉強は世界の情勢を理解する上で非常に重要であるが、名称や数字を暗記するのに終始し無味乾燥して学生の勉強がはかどらないことから、自分で多くの地理書を参照して編集した、とのことである。

参照した地理書として、*Encyclopedia Britanica, The Statesman's Yearbook, Longmans' Junior School Geography*, 米国「スウィントン」万国地理、Arnold Guyot 著 *Natural Geography* を挙げている。航海中の地

理に関する記述は杉森がもつ深い知識に基づいたものであった。

　英語による日記の記述が始まる2月4日から9月19日まではロンドンに滞在した。この期間は，英国での生活に慣れ，人間関係を確立した時期であった。ロンドンの多くの名所旧跡や博物館や美術館を訪れ，現地の学校を見学に行き，シェイクスピアの作品を始めとして多くの本を読み，英語の個人レッスンを受けている。日曜日は教会の礼拝に出席し日本人キリスト教徒の会に参加している。

　10月以降のオックスフォード滞在期間は，杉森が大学でHenry Sweetの音声学の講義に出席したことから最も注目に値する部分であろう。オックスフォード大学の正式な学生であった山崎宗直の「平田先生と牛津の思ひ出」によると，当時のオックスフォード大学の講義は，正式学生の邪魔にならない限り，当該講師の許可を得れば通常無料で聴講することができる，として，7名の英語及び英文学の教授の名をあげているが，杉森が講義を受けた以下の3名もその中に含まれている。

　　　English Literature (Professor) W. A. Raleigh, M. A, Fellow of Magdalen.
　　　Modern English Literature (Lecturer) E. de Selincourt, D. Litt., University.
　　　Phonetics. (Reader) Henry Sweet, M. A. Balliol.

日記中にも杉森が以下のように伝手を頼って，RaleighやSweet宛ての紹介状を書いてもらい聴講の許可を受けたことが記録されている（10月18日）。

　　　Called on Prof. Dyer, who had called in the morning when not in, and left notes of introduction to Profs. Raleigh & Sweet. He gave also a note of introduction to Mr. Whealer in Bodleian Library.

　Sweetの講義はその著書 *Practical Study of Languages* に基づいた内容であった。日記は英語で書かれているせいか淡々と短い記述に留まってお

り，講義の内容や感想などは見られない。

　前出の「英語教育批判会―中等学校英語教育の諸問題」の中で杉森は，「私はOxford大学に参りましてHenry Sweetの発音学の講義を聞くことにいたしました。まあこれでphoneticsの大体は諒解することができたのであります」とごく簡単に音声学をマスターしたかのように述べているが，ただ発音記号を覚えるだけで正しい発音が習得できるわけではなく，生の英語にふれることが大事であると考えているとして，スウィートの音声学の講義の後，下宿で子供たちと努めて話し，生の英語を勉強したとも語っている。

　杉森は熊本洋学校と東京築地一致英和学校（後の明治学院）で学び，若いころから英語音声については確かな能力を持ってはいたが，英国に来てその英語発音が通じないという体験をしている。ロンドンでもオックスフォードに来てからも，先生として適当な人物を探し，定期的に英会話のレッスンを受けている。スウィートの講義で学んだことを，現地での実践により修得しようとしたのかもしれない。

　留学の成果は帰国してからの広島高等師範学校での教育に生かされた。田邉氏は，前出の「日本英語音声教育史：杉森此馬の指導観」において，英語指導において文字中心となりがちな風潮を戒め，音声指導を中心に「真の英語（practicable practical English）」を教えるべきであるという考えを持っていたとしている。また，「日本英語音声教育史：P. A. SmithのNotes on Practical Phonetics. について」では，杉森によりオックスフォードで学んだ最先端の音声科学が広島高師に導入され，同校で「発音学」の実技面を担当した外国人教師P. A. Smithが残したNotes on Practical Phonetics. についても，杉森が持ち込んだSweet式の音声理論に基づいて，Smith独自の工夫を加えたものであろうと推測している。

　須貝清一や小原國芳を始めとする，杉森の教えを受け著名な英語教育者となった人々が杉森の授業についての回想として述べた内容が，松村氏による前出の「広島高等師範英語教授・杉森此馬」に数多く紹介されているが，「英国紳士のような風貌」「上品」「イギリス仕込みの発音」が共通に印象に残っているようだ。

『広島高等師範学校一覧』明治36年12月20日発行

役職		氏名
校長		北条時敬（ほうじょう・ときゆき）
教授	海外留学中	杉森此馬
	海外留学中	中目　覚（なかのめ・あきら）
	倫理　寮務課長	深田藤治（ふかだ・とうじ）
	英語　地理　法制経済	堀　卓次郎（ほり・たくじろう）
	歴史　本科地理歴史部主管 歴史家主任	新見吉治（しんみ・きちじ）
	兵式体操　体操科主任教授	雪吹熊次郎（いぶき・くまじろう）
	英語　本科英語部主幹 英語科主任教授	栗原　基（くりはら・もとい）
	国語	堀　維孝（ほり・いこう）
雇外国教師	英語	ウィルリアム・エリオット (William Elliott)
	英語	ピー・エー・スミス (P. A. Smith)
講師	英語	小日向定次郎（こびなた・さだじろう）

『広島高等師範学校一覧』明治37年11月13日発行

役職		氏名
校長		北条時敬（ほうじょう・ときゆき）
教授	海外留学中	杉森此馬
	海外留学中	中目　覚（なかのめ・あきら）
	倫理　寮務課長	深田藤治（ふかだ・とうじ）
	英語　地理　法制経済	堀　卓次郎（ほり・たくじろう）
	歴史　本科地理歴史部主管 歴史家主任	新見吉治（しんみ・きちじ）
	兵式体操　体操科主任教授	雪吹熊次郎（いぶき・くまじろう）
	英語　本科英語部主幹 農学	関　豊太郎（せき・とよたろう）
	英語　本科英語部主幹	栗原　基（くりはら・もとい）
	英語	小日向定次郎（こびなた・さだじろう）
	国語	堀　維孝（ほり・いこう）
雇外国教師	英語	ウィルリアム・エリオット (William Elliott)
	英語	ピー・エー・スミス (P. A. Smith)
講師	英語	菱沼平治（ひしぬま・へいじ）

山崎が「平田先生と牛津の思ひ出」の中で，彼の下宿の家族が杉森を「手紙の名人」と呼んでいたと書いているように，杉森は多くのはがきや書状のやりとりをしており，それを日記中の「発信」「受信」の欄に詳細に記録している。通信の相手は大まかには4つに分けられる。まず世話になった現地の人々や教会の牧師さんたち，それから報告書を送っている文部省とイギリスで親交を深めていた同じ文部省留学生や現地法人の日本人がいる。既に紹介した鈴木禎次，平田禿木の他に，戸田海市，内田銀蔵，永野武一郎，茨木清次郎，郵船会社の三本，三井物産倫敦支店の加地利夫，グラスゴーの磯野長蔵の名前が見られる。

　その他に妻のウメをはじめとする家族，そして従兄弟の白仁の名前も度々記録されている。さらに，継続的に連絡を取っている相手として，校長である北条時敬を始めとする広島高等師範学校（Hiroshima Normal Collegeを略してHNCと表記されている）の教員及びESSの学生たちである。この間，実際に学校で教鞭を取ってはいないが，ロンドンの書店から書籍やカタログを送る手配をする等，学校の英語教育に貢献しようとしていた。特に北条校長とは *The Times* や *The Daily Telegraph* の新聞や，戦争関係の写真雑誌等時事的な内容のものを頻繁にやり取りしているようである。

　杉森が渡航中の明治36年と明治37年の『広島高等師範学校一覧』から当時広島高師に在職していた校長及び教授職の教員たちさらに外国人教員や講師を抜き出すと左頁のようになり，多くの教員と通信していたことが確認できる。名前の読み方は日記中の表記と照合するために諸資料から編者がつけた。

杉森と鈴木禎次及び平田喜一（禿木）との交流

　杉森が，英国で多くの人々と円満な人間関係を築いていた様子が日記から読み取れるが，特に交流が深かった人物としては，ロンドン滞在中は鈴木禎次，オックスフォード滞在中は平田喜一（禿木）が挙げられるであろう。

鈴木禎次については瀬口哲夫著『名古屋を作った建築家・鈴木禎次』に詳しく述べられているが，明治26（1893）年帝国大学工科大学建築学科に入学し，主任教授の辰野金吾らから本格的な建築教育を受けた。明治38（1905）年の名古屋高等工業学校（現在の名古屋工業大学）の開校に備えて英国とフランスに留学し，帰国後は教授として同校に赴任した。現在名古屋工業大学には鈴木禎次賞が創設されている。鈴木は夏目漱石の妻の妹と結婚しており，夏目と義兄弟の間柄であった。夏目が明治33（1900）年から明治36（1903）年まで英国留学したのと入れ替わるように明治36年から留学した。夏目の「ロンドン日記」にも鈴木の名前が何度か出ている。
　杉森の最初の下宿は最寄り駅がハムステッドで，和田博文他著『言語都市・ロンドン1861-1945』（藤原書店）によると日本人が多く居住した閑静な住宅地であった。そして杉森が住んだStanley Gardens 44は鈴木の下宿Stanley Gardens 51と同じ町内である。夏目を通じた縁からなのかは不明であるが，鈴木が杉森の下宿を手配した可能性もあるであろう。
　杉森がロンドンに到着し下宿に落ち着いた翌日1月28日に鈴木を訪問し，ロンドンの事情を聞き，一緒に市内見学に出かけている。2月には共にオックスフォードに出かけ，次に述べる平田喜一の案内でカレッジや名所旧跡を訪問している。8月にはニューカッスルオンタインに小旅行に出かけたが，途中で鈴木も合流し，共にダーラムの建築物を見学している。9月に杉森はロンドンからオックスフォードに移ったが，その時期も書状のやり取りは続いた。
　なお，「INAX　REPORT No.180　続・生き続ける建築—2　鈴木禎次」では，鈴木の建築物や図面の画像が見られる。
　平田喜一については，福原麟太郎（編）『平田禿木追憶』に多くの人からの追悼文，略伝，著作目録がまとめられている。
　平田は明治23（1890）年に第一高等中学校に入った。文学に傾倒し，文芸には「禿木」という名前を使っていた。英語が堪能であったことから東京高師英語専修科に入学し直し，卒業後東京高師付属中学で，数年後には東京高等師範学校で英語を教えた。帰朝後は東京高師の教壇に戻ったが，徐々に英語教育からは離れ，随筆執筆や英文学翻訳に専心した。

平田は杉森より1年前にオックスフォードに来ていた。平田は当時30歳代の始めで，後の文芸評論家・劇作家島村抱月他の同年代の日本人留学生内田銀蔵，山崎宗直，好本督らと親しくしていたことが知られている。島村抱月がベルリンに去った直後に杉森はオックスフォードに来ており，ストラットフォード・オン・エイボンに小旅行に出かけたり，度々一緒に *The Sketch Book* の読書をするなど親しく交流した。

オックスフォードにおける平田については，小林信行氏の「イギリスにおける平田禿木（1）」「イギリスにおける平田禿木（2）」により，主に当時の文芸誌に投稿された随筆と友人知人への書簡に基づいて，詳細な研究が行われている。ただ，平田の留学中の綿密な日記類は見つかっていないとされていることから，杉森の日記が平田に関する補完的な資料となる可能性があると思われる。

平田が文芸誌「古古路乃華」に掲載した「牛津より」と杉森の日記の内容が一致している部分を紹介する。次は杉森の5月21日の日記である。

> Stratford-on-Avon. In the morning went to Shakespeare's Birthplace again & saw the librarian Mr. Richard Savage who showed us several manuscripts & took us (Dr. Jacob Ritter, an Austrian, Mr. Kiichi Hirata & myself) to Anne Hathaway's Cottage, where the great poet used to court for his future wife. Saw many old things. On leaving Miss Anne Hathaway Baker (she is named after old Anne Hathaway) the daughter of the man who looks after the Cottage picked twigs of the rosemary growing close to the cottage & gave it to each of us as a memory of our visit.（後略）

日記から次のことが読み取れる。5月21日は雨で，その時の道連れが同宿のオーストリア人 Dr. Jacob Ritter と Mr. Kiichi Hirata であった。一行は，シェイクスピアの生家（Shakespeare's Birthplace）を訪れ，Librarian の Mr. Richard Savage に案内されて，シェイクスピアが将来の妻となる Anne Hathaway に求婚した「アン・ハサウェイの家（Anne Hathaway's

解説　277

Cottage)」を訪問する。そこで，アン・ハサウェイの名を取って名づけられた少女（Anne Hathaway Baker）から，訪問の記念にローズマリーをもらう。

次に平田の「牛津より」からストラットフォード訪問の部分を以下に示す。

　　　　ことし五月沙翁の郷ストラトフオゝドに遊び
　　　　その妻なる人の旧家を訪ひしに案内の娘雨に
　　　　ぬれつゝ庭なるロオズ，ソレエをつみて与え
　　　　　　ければ（二）
　　　シド子リイが案内の書にはさまんか
　　　　　　　　雨につみにし君がこの花
　　　シド子リイがストラトフオオドの小記こよな
　　　　　　き手引きに候
　　　我もまたアン，ハザウェと名をつげて
　　　　　　　　後の井リアム待ち給うか君
　　　　　　何代の高尾などいふ如く独りをかしく思ひ候

　前半では，5月に沙翁（シェイクスピア）の故郷ストラットフォードを訪問し，Anne Hathaway の家を訪ねたことが記され，当日が雨であったこと，案内の娘が「ローズ，ソレエ（Mary を表すメレエか？）」を摘んでくれたことが読み取れる。「シド子リイが案内の書」とは，Sidney Lee の著作 *Stratford-on-Avon* を指していると推測される。同書にはこの町の起源や歴史，風物などが Edward Hull による美しい多くのイラストと一緒に記されている。「アン・ハサウェイの家」の紹介部分には，エリザベス王朝時代を思わせるこの美しい家やシェイクスピアが将来の妻に求婚した "Shakespeare's courting chair" について記されている。後半では，ウィリアム・シェイクスピアの妻となった Anne Hathaway の名前をとって名づけられた娘について，君も初代の Anne Hathaway と同様にこの家で将来の夫となる人を待っているのかと詠い，また代々名前が襲名された高尾太夫のようであると述べている。

この2つの文章は内容が細かいところまで一致しており，特に平田の文の意味は，杉森の日記の記述により，よりよく理解できる。
　秋になり大学が始まる時期になると，9月19日に杉森はロンドンからオックスフォードに移っている。同日平田を訪ね，「26 Richmond St.」にいったん下宿を決めているが，9月20日，21日と平田を訪ね，9月22日には下宿を「Woolmer House, 46 South-moor Rd.」に変えている。この住所は，川副國基著『島村抱月の渡英滞英日記について』において島村抱月の下宿の住所とされているものと同一である。島村抱月は7月にドイツのベルリンに発っており，そこを平田が杉森に紹介したとも考えられるであろう。小林信行著「イギリスにおける平田禿木（2）」には，平田が初めてオックスフォードに来たときには，抱月が好本に依頼して平田の下宿を世話したことが記されており，当時の日本人留学生同士の支えあいが伺える部分である。
　10月に入ると，オックスフォード大学に毎日聴講に行く生活と，平田とほとんど毎日お互いを訪問しあって一緒に同じ本（*The Sketch Book*）を読んでいる様子が読み取れる。読書後にどのような感想を話し合ったのかは記されてはいないが，回を重ねて行われた二人だけの読書会は，その後多くの西洋文学の翻訳を国民文庫研究会から出版した平田の解釈に杉森も何らかの影響を与え，杉森も文学者平田の才能に触れる機会となったであろう。

参考文献

安部規子（2015）.「修猷館の英語教育―明治時代の英語教師（5）杉森此馬について―」『久留米工業高等専門学校紀要』31(1),1-10.

安部規子（2018）.「広島高等師範学校教授・杉森此馬の英国留学―オックスフォードでの平田喜一（禿木）との交流を中心に―」『英学史研究』51，85－101.

伊地知純正（1918）.『倫敦名所図会』研究社

「INAX REPORT No.180　続・生き続ける建築―2　鈴木禎次」https://www.bizlixil.com / resource / pic / column / inaxreport / IR180/IR180_p04-16.pdf（参照 2017-5-1）

川副國基（1951）.『島村抱月の渡英滞英日記について』早稲田大学教育会研究叢書第二冊

小林信行（2006）.「イギリスにおける平田禿木（1）」『英学史研究』39,97-115.

小林信行（2013）.「イギリスにおける平田禿木（2）」『英学史研究』46,18-28.

杉森此馬（1893）.『政治天然万国地理提要』丸善株式会社書店

杉森此馬（1907）.「英語の学習に就きて」『余は如何にして英語を学びしか　附如何にして英語を学ぶべきか』62-65, 有楽社

杉森此馬（1909a）.「牛津略記」広島高等師範学校教育研究会（編）『教育研究会講演集』[第3冊] 第4集，136-142, 金港堂.

杉森此馬（1909b）.「英国教育の一斑」『福岡縣教育会々報』135,7-19.

杉森此馬他（1932）.「英語教育批判会―中等学校英語教育の諸問題―」『英語英文学論叢』2(1),90-211.

杉森百年史編集委員会編（1995）.『杉森百年史』杉森女子高等学校

瀬口哲夫（2004）.『名古屋をつくった建築家・鈴木禎次』名古屋 CD フォーラム

田邊祐司（2010）.「日本英語音声教育史：杉森此馬の指導観」『英学史論叢』13,13-26.

田邊祐司（2018）.「日本英語音声教育史：P. A. Smith の Notes on Practical Phonetics. について」『専修人文論集』102,23-42.

辻直人（2010）.『近代日本海外留学の目的変容―文部省留学生の派遣実態について―』東信堂.

野上豊一郎（1941）.『西洋見学』日本評論社

平岡敏夫（編）（1990）.「ロンドン日記」『漱石日記』岩波書店

平田禿木（1904）.「牛津より」『古古路乃華』8(9),32-33.

平田禿木（1918）.「オックスフォードの思出」『大學及大學生』14, 107-111.

平田諭治（1997）.「岡倉由三郎ロンドン大学講演考―背景と経緯―」『英学史研究』30, 47-59.

平田諭治（1998）.「岡倉由三郎の渡米＜日本＞講演」『英学史研究』31, 97-110.

平田諭治（2018）.「1901年度文部省外国留学生としての岡倉由三郎：ヨーロッパ留学の背景・経緯とその実際」『筑波大学教育学系論集』42(2),1-13.
「広島高等師範学校一覧　明治36年から38年」国立国会図書館デジタルコレクション http://dl.ndl.go.jp/info:ndljp／pid/813333/67（参照 2018-12-24）
福原麟太郎（1941）.「平田禿木伝」『福原麟太郎（編）『平田禿木追悼』140-144.
福原麟太郎（編）（1943）.「平田禿木著作目録」福原麟太郎（編）『平田禿木追悼』145-165.
松村幹男（1977）.「広島高師の外国人教師―Elliot, Smith および Pringle―」『英学史研究』10,51-59.
松村幹男（1996）.「広島高等師範英語教授・杉森此馬」『英學史會報』19，3－12.
文部省専門学務局「明治三十六年三月三十一日調　文部省外国留学生表」国会図書館デジタルアーカイブ http://dl.ndl.go.jp/info:ndljp/pid/809313（参照2017-5-1）
山崎宗直（1943）.「平田先生と牛津の思ひ出」福原麟太郎（編）『平田禿木追悼』93-94.
渡辺村男（著）　柳川山門三池教育会（編）（1980）.『旧柳川藩志（全）』青潮社
和田博文・真鍋正宏・西村将洋・宮内淳子・和田桂子（2009）.『言語都市・ロンドン1861－1945』藤原書店

Irving, W. (1819-20). *The Sketch Book of Geoffrey Crayon, Gent.*
Lee, S. (1890). *Stratford-on-Avon*. Cambridge University Press.
Sugimori, K. (1907a). Talks on Pronunciation I. *The English Teachers' Magazine*, 1(1), 20-22.
Sugimori, K. (1907b). Talks on Pronunciation II. *The English Teachers' Magazine*, 1(3), 21-25.
Sweet, H. (1900). *The Practical Study of Languages*. Henry Holt and Company.

あとがき

安部規子

　平成27（2015）年3月，髙月三世子氏から杉森此馬の遺品が柳川古文書館に寄贈されることをうかがいました。杉森此馬は私にとって，旧制の福岡県立中学修猷館の卓越した英語教師の1人（在職期間：明治27年7月～明治29年5月）ではありましたが，主要な業績は広島高等師範学校の教授としてのものであり，広島大学名誉教授でいらした故松村幹男先生が深く研究されておられ，また，英語音声教育の面からは専修大学教授・田邉祐司先生が現在でも研究しておられることから，私がさらに研究できることは残されていないように思っておりました。

　しかし，日記のデジタルデータをところどころ読んでいると，100年前のものであるにもかかわらず大変おもしろく，1月分，また1月分と続けて読んでいました。年頭に詠まれた歌にこめられた郷愁や留学への決意，日露戦争勃発直前という緊迫した時期の航海中の船内の様子，航路上にある各地の地理的な特徴，マルセイユ上陸時の感想やちょっとした事件，英国の風物や伝統文化，オックスフォード大学での学究生活や産業革命による工業化，そこに暮らす日本人の生活など，当時の日本人留学生の多くが経験したことであろうと思われ，これを何かの形にして多くの方に紹介したいと考えるようになりました。

　日記の解読は日本語部分の方がむしろ英語よりも難しく，漢字とカタカナで書かれてはいても，くずし字が多用された100年前の日本語は私の手には負えないものでした。この作業においては，所蔵先である柳川古文書館学芸員の江島香氏に大変多くのご教示をいただきました。また，同館の柳川市市史編さん係学芸員嘱託伊東かおり氏にも，留学中に撮影された杉森の写真について貴重な調査結果をご教示いただきました。英語部分の解読作業には豊福真弓氏，黒木直子氏にご助力いただきましたが，いくつか

の部分は判読不可能のままとなりました。Frank Carbullido 氏には，私が読み取れない部分を何箇所も解読していただいたばかりでなく，本書の意義についても貴重な教示をいただきました。

　Carbullido 氏は，ラフカディオ・ハーンが描く日本を日本人が興味深く読むように，日本人の目からみた当時の英国の様子には英国人やその他の国の人々も興味を覚えるだろう，と述べられ，その言葉で，英語部分のみを日本人のために翻訳するという当初の計画を変更し，日本語部分も同時に英語に翻訳することにしました。

　翻訳は全て私自身で行いましたが，日英の翻訳では，Carbullido 氏が杉森の簡潔な英文のスタイルと統一感がでるように，私の英語を手直ししてくれました。最終的には，黒上英子氏が日英・英日両方の翻訳全体に目を通し推敲してくれました。ご教示，ご助力下さった方々に感謝いたします。誠にありがとうございました。

　本書には Sidney Lee 著 *Stratford-on-Avon*（Cambridge University Press, 1890）から Edward Hull によるイラストを，伊地知純正著『倫敦名所図会』（研究社, 1918）から写真を引用させていただきました。また，当時のロンドンの風物に関して，和田博文他著『言語都市・ロンドン　1861 − 1945』から多くの示唆を受けました。

　杉森が見ていた風景をこの目で確認したいという気持ちで，平成30 (2018) 年の 8 月に黒上英子氏とともに英国へ飛び（船旅は無理でした），ロンドン，ストラットフォード・オン・エイボン，ウォリック，レミントン・スパ，オックスフォードなどに杉森の足跡を訪ねました。ロンドンでは杉森がよく散歩していたハムステッド・ヒースやプリムローズ・ヒルを歩き，ストラットフォードではシェイクスピアの生家やアン・ハサウェイの家を巡り，シェイクスピア劇を鑑賞しました。ウォリックでは，12月29日に杉森がしたようにセント・メアリー教会の塔に登り町を一望し，ウォリック城を見学しました。オックスフォードではボドリアン図書館ツアーに参加するとともに，杉森が日曜日の礼拝に通っていたマンスフィールド・カレッジのチャペル（現在は食堂としても使われている）を見学することができました。

英国では100年以上たっても多くのものが当時のままに残っており，杉森が訪れた場所を，私たちも同じように経験することができたのは幸せなことでした。12月27日に杉森がロイヤル・パンプ・ルームで入浴したレミントン・スパはかつて温泉保養地として有名でした。現在では入浴施設はなくなっていますが，建物はそのまま残っており，中の小さな博物館でその歴史を知ることができました。

　今回の旅が，杉森の時代はもちろん20年前と比べても大きく異なっていたのは，インターネットの普及でした。かつてのように行く先々でまずインフォメーションに立ち寄り，カウンターの人から地図を入手する代わりに，今回はWiFiを持ち歩き，スマートフォンのアプリを駆使して目的地へのルートを検索したり，列車の切符を購入したり，芝居のお得なチケットを取ったりしましたが，WiFiとスマートフォンなしには限られた日数の中で杉森の足跡をたどることは難しかったでしょう。また，スマートフォン以上に私たちを助けてくれたのは，当時ウォリック大学の在外研究員であった田中彰則氏でした。田中氏は，杉森と同じ福岡県柳川市の出身であることもあってか，私たちを気遣い現地の情報を種々提供してくれただけでなく，研究の合間を縫って目的地に同行してくれた時もありました。オックスフォードでのパンティング（川下り）では，柳川での船頭さんの経験を生かして平底船を操ってくれた他，度々パブにも付き合って下さり，楽しい時間を共にすることができました。心から感謝しています。

　日記の寄贈者である髙月三世子氏にはお祖父様である杉森此馬とご家族について多くのことを教えていただきました。日記中に英国で紅茶はよく飲んでいるが，パブには出かけたという記述がないことをお伝えすると，祖父は決してお酒を口にしない人でした，とのお返事をいただきました。

　本書により，杉森の日本の英語教育への貢献とともにそのまじめで誠実な人柄や友人関係に関しても知られるようになれば幸いです。

　最後に海鳥社の西俊明氏は本書の出版を快く引き受けて下さいました。ありがとうございました。

2019年3月16日

編者・安部規子(あべ・のりこ) 広島大学大学院教育学研究科修了、博士(教育学)。久留米工業高等専門大学校教授。著書に『修猷館の英語教育 明治編』(海鳥社、2012年)がある。

杉森此馬英国留学日記
明治37年1月1日−12月31日
A Japanese Scholar's 1904 Diary in the UK.
編者 安部規子

■

2019年5月17日 第一刷発行

■

発行者 杉本雅子
発行所 有限会社海鳥社
〒812−0023 福岡市博多区奈良屋町13番4号
電話092(272)0120 FAX092(272)0121
http://www.kaichosha-f.co.jp
印刷・製本 有限会社九州コンピュータ印刷
ISBN978-4-86656-051-9
［定価は表紙カバーに表示］